caprial's

SOUPS & Sandwiches

caprial's

SOUPS
&
Sandwiches

CAPRIAL PENCE *and* MARK DOWERS

Ten Speed Press
Berkeley, California

Special thanks to those who kindly loaned props:
Carl Greve for the photographs on pages 24, 28,
32, 54, 94, and 112; Heather Bowen for the
photographs on pages 20, 36, 46, 50, 78, 82, 100,
104, and 108; Patrick Horsley for the photograph
on page 86.

Ten Speed Press
P.O. Box 7123
Berkeley, California 94707
www.tenspeed.com

Distributed in Australia by Simon and Schuster
Australia, in Canada by Ten Speed Press Canada,
in New Zealand by Tandem Press, in South Africa
by Real Books, in Southeast Asia by Berkeley
Books, and in the United Kingdom and Europe by
Airlift Books.

Cover and text design by Toni Tajima.
Writing assistance by Jennifer Morrison,
        Portland, Oregon.
Food photography by Edward Gowans,
        Portland, Oregon.
Front cover photo and location photography by
        Jerome Hart, Portland, Oregon.
Food styling by Heather Bowen, Portland, Oregon,
        assisted by Meg Graves Talbott.

Library of Congress Cataloging-in-Publication Data
Pence, Caprial.
    [Soups and sandwiches]
    Caprial's soups and sandwiches / by Caprial
Pence and Mark Dowers.
        p.   cm.
    Includes index.
    ISBN 1-58008-025-1
    1. Soups. 2. Sandwiches. I. Dowers, Mark.
    II. Title.
TX757.P46   1999
641.8'13--dc21   98-38815
                                        CIP

First printing 1998
Printed in China

1 2 3 4 5 6 7 8 9 10 — 02 01 00 99 98

To the Bistro staff, especially John Mannenbach and Mark,
for all you do for John and me.

—Caprial Pence

To my mom, who gave me the gift of cooking.

—Mark Dowers

Contents

Acknowledgments

FROM CAPRIAL AND MARK, thanks to Kevin Barnes, David Robertson, Shannon Chasteen, Marianne Ogura, and all our friends who helped with the recipe testing and tasting; to John Mannenbach, Chris Gooch, Jeff Welton, and all our staff at the Bistro; to Jenny Morrison for helping to put words in our mouths; to our families for all their support; to Ed Gowans, Jerry Hart, and Heather Bowen for the wonderful photography and food styling; and to Lorena Jones, Aaron Wehner, and Toni Tajima at Ten Speed Press for all their work in creating a great book. From Mark, thanks also to Caprial and John Pence, and Chuck Stewart, who helped make this book possible for me.

DURING LUNCH AT CAPRIAL'S BISTRO—the restaurant I co-own with my husband, John—the pace is quicker and the atmosphere more casual than at dinner. We see many of our regular customers at this time of day. For these familiar faces, lunch at the Bistro just isn't right unless they order a certain dish. Although we change our menu every month, to keep these special folks happy a few items never stray from the menu: the marinated eggplant sandwich, the hot-as-hell chicken, the spinach salad with Asian black bean dressing, and the Bistro burger. The Bistro's lunch ambiance is the perfect setting for a sandwich or a bowl of soup, the two menu items that *really* command an encore presentation, especially for our regulars who come in for lunch three or four times a week. Of course, plain old ham and Swiss or chicken noodle soup won't keep Bistro enthusiasts coming back for more. Our customers expect a daily sandwich special

that has a creative, flavorful twist, like roast turkey on sundried tomato and basil challah with aioli and arugula, or Asian-style barbecued pork served with grilled onions on a French roll. As for our soup of the day, many of our regulars come in specifically for our latest creation. They know it will be a great bowl of soup, thanks to our chef, Mark Dowers, who takes the art of soup-making to lofty levels.

Mark started working for us at the Bistro five years ago as our day cook, the person in charge of the lunch service. For his inaugural duty, we asked him to make the soup for lunch. I'll never forget my first whiff of the delicious soup he created: a sweet potato soup with chorizo sausage and cinnamon croutons. The combination of velvety puréed sweet potatoes, piquant chorizo, and crunchy, spicy-sweet croutons was one of the best flavor mixtures I'd ever tasted, and the customers loved it, too. After that tasty introduction to Mark's gift for blending flavors (some of his combinations sound unusual at first, but they always taste wonderful), we immediately assigned him all soup-making duties. An amazing array of soups began to emerge from the kitchen, and soon Mark had no choice but to humbly accept the nickname "Soup God." With our talented day cook thus anointed and hard at work, the Bistro's lunch crowd continued to grow. Mark was promoted to head chef, and our customers' enthusiastic response attests to his skill and creativity.

The Bistro's reputation for fantastic soups and sandwiches, plus the popularity and long-standing tradition of these two perennial favorites, inspired us to write this book. It just seemed natural that Mark and I should share our recipes and tips with others. The subject may seem rather focused, but consider that the best soups and sandwiches aren't just for lunch, meant to be eaten in a hurry during a break from work. These recipes will open up endless possibilities for meals served out on the patio, in front of the fireplace, in the dining room on your best dishes, or under a tree on a picnic blanket. Don't think that homemade soup or an interesting sandwich equals too many hours in a hot kitchen—I don't have that kind of time, either! Those ideal elements, homemade stocks and breads, aren't difficult to make, and they taste wonderful. But by all means go for a shortcut if it means the difference between preparing one of these recipes and popping a frozen pizza in the oven.

Whether we're developing a new menu for the Bistro or coming up with something different to cook in our homes, Mark and I both like to go about it with a sense of adventure. Although we have the confidence that comes from formal training as chefs and years of working in restaurants, there's absolutely no reason that your creative cooking process can't be the same as ours. For example, we consider the weather. Is it gloomy? Perfect for bright Asian and tropical flavors! We have such a great time wandering the aisles of local ethnic markets, scanning the packages, jars, and bottles for new, exotic seasonings and ingredients to try. Often the inspiration is much closer to home, when a simple peek into the refrigerator or pantry will reveal what needs to be eaten up. We love to read cookbooks and food magazines of all kinds to see what other cooks are up to. Classic old cookbooks and used-bookstore treasures can provide just the right starting point for developing a new twist on a traditional dish, as Mark did with his spoonbread recipe.

Our favorite way to create a recipe, though, is to look at everything the season holds. Each change in the season means something new and exciting you can cook with. Here in Oregon this means Dungeness crab and Hubbard, butternut, and acorn squash in the winter; crisp, peppery watercress and tender asparagus in the spring; sweet, luscious strawberries in early summer; huge, pristine bundles of basil and beautiful vine-ripened tomatoes during the heat of summer. And during the fall, when the harvest is in full swing, our Willamette Valley farmers stay busy picking wine grapes, corn, beans, pumpkins, and more. (I always plan a harvest dinner to celebrate this particular time of year.) Enliven your own creativity by shopping at your local farmers' market, where the produce is fresh from the farm and you can talk face to face with the grower. You'll come home and want to head straight to the kitchen. Mark even gets calls at the Bistro from local farmers who give him lists of available produce. It might mean changing the menu he planned to prepare, but he quickly comes up with a new dish that takes advantage of the fresh ingredients.

In this book, you'll find twenty-five soup recipes and twenty-five sandwich recipes. In addition, we've included master recipes for stocks and breads, along with an array of recipes for garnishes, spreads, and assorted toppings that can be mixed and matched with both soups and sandwiches—not to mention anything else that sounds good to you. Rounding out the book is a basics section that covers some kitchen fundamentals and a glossary of terms and ingredients for easy reference.

We developed all of the recipes in our home kitchens, using simplified versions of the techniques we use in the restaurant, and tested them with our families and friends. Try them out for yourself. It's my hope that this book will give you a starting point for developing the same love of food and combinations of flavors that Mark and I share.

STOCKS & Such

Nothing beats coming inside on a cold day and breathing in the comforting aroma of garlic, herbs, and vegetables simmering in stock on the stove. Around the world, from rustic cooking fires to utterly modern kitchens, soup—in its most simple sense, meat, vegetables, or fish cooked in liquid— has always satisfied. Soup is versatile, simple, healthful, convenient, and economical. It can be a crystal-clear, intensely flavored con- sommé served as just one course of many in a special dinner, or it can be a homey one-pot meal of vegetables, meat, and beans in a hearty broth. Today we're lucky to have easy access to an international array of ingredients and recipes, making the soup pot the perfect place to draw together a mix of cultural influ- ences and flavors.

At the Bistro, we like to play with different flavors and steer clear of common dishes, and our soups reflect this philosophy. Like many home cooks, we often don't have the time to prepare soups that require long, intensive processes. Mark's soups are innovative and exotic, or traditional with a twist, and he prefers quicker preparations that work well for the home cook.

You can't go wrong by serving soup as the focus of a meal; a loaf of good bread and a fresh green salad make dinner complete. In fact, when Mark throws a dinner party at home, soup is almost always the star attraction. For him, each recipe inspires a different serving idea. He'll serve chicken soup in vintage bowls or fill souvenir coconut-shell bowls with his Spicy Peanut Soup with Curry and Vegetables (page 39).

If you serve soup as one of several courses, make sure its flavors and heaviness match the rest of the meal. For example, you wouldn't want to serve contrasting flavors like a potato-leek soup with a Thai dinner, and a creamy seafood bisque followed by a heavy, rich pasta would overwhelm even the boldest appetites. On the other hand, Chanterelle Velvet (page 19) served with grilled chicken is an excellent pairing, especially if you serve it with a nice Pinot Noir.

Soups are the perfect dish for practicing variations. For example, our basic potato purée starts with potatoes simmered in stock. When the purée is prepared with a chicken stock, we might add a mushroom duxelles and toasted hazelnuts, whereas with an asparagus stock, we might garnish it with asparagus tips and watercress.

On a more practical note, soup is often better the second day. If you have leftover soup, store it in a clean container and refrigerate it right away. Reheat soup very gently, either on the stove over low heat or in the microwave. Most soups will keep several days, but if you're making soup that contains seafood, it's best to make just enough for one meal; most types of seafood don't reheat well.

Although soup is a great dish to make when it comes to improvising, it's helpful to understand the various types of soups and their traditional definition or method of preparation.

Broth-Based Soup As the name suggests, this is a soup prepared with broth—meat, bones, vegetables, or all three, simmered in water or stock. Mediterranean Vegetable Soup (page 97) and Chicken with Noodles and Herbs (page 22) both fall under this multipurpose category.

Bisque These days, a range of creamy soups are mistakenly called "bisques," but the real thing is a shellfish soup flavored with the essence of the crushed shells and thickened with a roux.

Chowder With its roots in the American East Coast, chowder's primary elements are bacon or salt pork, potatoes, fish or chicken stock, fresh seafood or vegetables, and usually cream. Mark likes to make smoked seafood and corn variations, and sometimes thickens chowder with mashed potatoes.

Purée One puréed main ingredient, such as a legume or vegetable, characterizes this type of soup. The purée is finished with stock and seasonal flavors. Purées can range from a hearty bean soup to a light and refreshing roasted pepper purée.

Stew Traditionally a stew consists of meat cut into bite-sized pieces and braised with vegetables until fork tender. At the Bistro, our stews might be curried lamb or bourguignonne-style beef stew, as well as seafood stews like bouillabaisse and gumbo.

Always remember that, in addition to quality stocks, using the freshest ingredients will reward you with memorable soup every time!

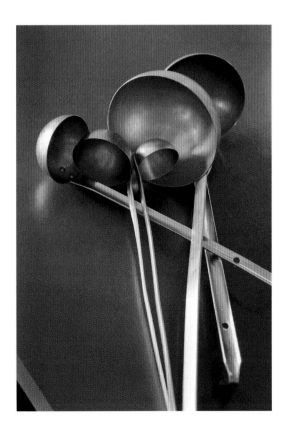

stocks

Even if your personal soup-making experience is limited to opening a can and measuring out the water, you can easily learn the basics. Always start with a quality stock, preferably homemade. Stocks can take up to several hours to simmer, but their preparation is extremely easy. There is no need to hover in the kitchen; simply combine the ingredients, add cold water, and let your stove do the rest.

Freeze perfectly good stock ingredients that you otherwise might throw away, like chicken carcasses, crab, shrimp, and lobster shells, beef bones, and the ends of celery and carrots. When the mood strikes, make a few batches of stock and freeze them, so you'll always be ready to create a flavorful soup. To do so, first cool the freshly made stock in a shallow container in the refrigerator. Then transfer it for freezing into several two-quart heavy-duty plastic zip-top bags or plastic containers.

chicken or turkey stock

Yield: About 1 quart

- 2 pounds chicken or turkey bones, rinsed
- 2 onions, coarsely chopped
- 2 carrots, coarsely chopped
- 2 stalks celery, coarsely chopped
- 3 cloves garlic, chopped
- 4 sprigs thyme
- 8 cups water
- 1 bay leaf

In a large stockpot over high heat, bring the bones, onions, carrots, celery, garlic, thyme, and water just to boil. Add the bay leaf. Reduce the heat and simmer for 4 to 6 hours, or until the stock is richly flavored. Strain through a fine sieve into a bowl and use immediately, or let cool to room temperature before refrigerating.

This stock keeps in the refrigerator for up to one week and can be frozen.

Note: To make **strong chicken stock**, reduce the stock over high heat until about 2 cups remain and the flavor has intensified.

beef, veal, or lamb stock

Yield: About 1 quart

- 5 pounds beef, veal, or lamb bones
- 2 onions, coarsely chopped
- 1 carrot, coarsely chopped
- 3 stalks celery, coarsely chopped
- 3 cloves garlic, chopped
- 2 tablespoons tomato paste
- 1 cup dry red wine
- 8 cups water
- 1 bay leaf

Preheat the oven to 450°. Place the bones, onions, carrot, celery, and garlic in a roasting pan, and roast for about 1 hour, or until the bones turn golden brown. Spread the tomato paste over the mixture and roast for 10 more minutes. Transfer the mixture to a large stockpot. Add the wine to the roasting pan and, with a wooden spoon, scrape up all of the brown bits from the bottom of the pan. Pour this liquid into the stockpot. Add the water and bay leaf. Bring to a boil over high heat. Reduce the heat and simmer for 6 to 8 hours, or until the stock is full flavored. Strain through a fine sieve into a bowl and use immediately, or let cool to room temperature before refrigerating.

This stock keeps in the refrigerator for up to 1 week and can be frozen.

Note: To make **rich beef, veal, or lamb stock**, reduce the stock over high heat until 2 cups remain and the flavor has intensified.

vegetable stock

Yield: About 1 quart

- 3 onions, coarsely chopped
- 4 carrots, coarsely chopped
- 5 stalks celery, coarsely chopped
- 4 ounces mushrooms, coarsely chopped
- 4 cloves garlic, chopped
- 3 shallots, chopped
- 6 sprigs thyme
- 8 cups water

In a large stockpot over high heat, bring all the ingredients just to a boil. Reduce the heat and simmer for about 1 hour, or until the stock is full flavored. Strain through a fine sieve into a bowl and use immediately, or let cool to room temperature before refrigerating.

This stock keeps in the refrigerator for up to 1 week and can be frozen.

Note: To make **roasted vegetable stock**, place all the vegetables in a large baking dish and roast in a 425° oven for 20 minutes. Add the roasted vegetables to the stockpot of boiling water and proceed as directed above.

fish stock
Yield: About 1 quart

- 1 pound fish bones (use bones from white fish only)
- 1 tablespoon unsalted butter
- 2 leeks, white part only, rinsed well and coarsely chopped
- 2 large onions, coarsely chopped
- 2 stalks celery, coarsely chopped
- 2 cloves garlic, chopped
- $1/4$ cup mushroom stems
- 1 cup dry white wine
- 4 sprigs thyme
- 8 cups water

Coarsely chop the fish bones and place them in a large bowl or stockpot. Cover with cold water and soak for 1 to 2 hours to remove any remaining traces of blood. Drain.

In a large stockpot over high heat, melt the butter until bubbling. Add the leeks, onions, celery, garlic, and mushroom stems, and sauté until fragrant, 3 to 4 minutes. Add the wine and bones, decrease the heat, cover the pot, and sweat the mixture for about 8 minutes. Add the thyme and water and simmer, uncovered, for 25 minutes more. Strain through a fine sieve into a bowl and use immediately, or let cool to room temperature before refrigerating.

This stock keeps in the refrigerator for up to 1 week and can be frozen.

seafood stock
Yield: About 1 quart

- 2 leeks
- 1 tablespoon unsalted butter
- 2 large onions, coarsely chopped
- 2 stalks celery, coarsely chopped
- 2 cloves garlic, chopped
- $1/4$ cup mushroom stems
- 1 cup dry white wine
- 6 cups shrimp, crab, or lobster shells
- 4 sprigs thyme
- 2 quarts water

Discard the green portion of the leeks. Trim and rinse the white parts thoroughly, then coarsely chop. In a large stockpot over high heat, melt the butter until bubbling. Add the leeks, onions, celery, garlic, and mushroom stems, and sauté until they become aromatic, 3 to 4 minutes. Add the wine and shells, decrease the heat, cover the pot, and sweat the mixture for about 8 minutes. Add the thyme and water and simmer, uncovered, for 25 minutes more. Strain through a fine sieve into a bowl and use immediately, or let cool to room temperature before refrigerating.

This stock keeps in the refrigerator for up to 1 week and can be frozen.

...and such

The garnishes that Mark uses are an important component in every soup he makes. The following recipes are some of the more versatile toppings we use at the Bistro to add depth and flair to soups. The purées and tapenade work well with both simple dishes like a grilled chicken sandwich and more complicated fare like the Stuffed Portobello Mushroom Sandwich (page 77).

spicy cinnamon croutons

Makes 4 cups

Croutons and crostini lend themselves best to hearty purée soups such as Sweet Potato and Caramelized Onion Soup (page 53) and Bistro Potato Soup (page 55).

¹/₄ cup butter
1 cup firmly packed brown sugar
1 teaspoon chile powder
1 teaspoon ground cinnamon
1 baguette or loaf of sourdough bread,
  cut into ¹/₄-inch cubes

Preheat the oven to 375°. Melt the butter in a sauté pan over medium heat. Stir in the brown sugar, chile powder, and cinnamon, and cook 2 to 3 minutes, or until bubbly. Transfer to a large bowl. Add the bread and toss to evenly coat. Spread the croutons on a sheet pan and bake until crispy and caramelized, 25 to 30 minutes. Remove the croutons from the oven and cool on a wire rack. (Don't worry if they stick together— they will break apart as they cool.)

rosemary croutons

Makes 4 cups

1 baguette or loaf of sourdough bread,
  cut into ¹/₄-inch cubes
¹/₄ cup butter
1 tablespoon chopped fresh rosemary
3 cloves garlic, minced

Preheat the oven to 375°. Place the bread cubes in a in a medium-size bowl. In a sauté pan over medium heat, melt the butter with the rosemary and garlic. Pour the mixture over the bread cubes and toss well. Spread the croutons on a sheet pan and bake until golden brown, 10 to 15 minutes.

crostini

Makes about 20 slices

1 baguette, sliced on the diagonal into
  ¹/₂-inch slices
¹/₄ cup olive oil
4 cloves garlic, minced

Preheat the oven to 350°. In a small bowl, combine the olive oil and garlic. Place the bread slices on a sheet pan and drizzle with the olive oil mixture. Bake the crostini until golden brown, about 10 minutes.

scallion-roquefort croustades

Makes about 20 slices

The tang of the blue cheese and the crispness of the croustades makes a nice addition to the sweet flavors of the Onion Soup (page 58). Also try the croustades with the creamy Bistro Potato Soup (page 55).

- 3 bunches scallions, green part only, chopped
- 8 ounces blue cheese
- 1 teaspoon chopped fresh tarragon
- 1 baguette, sliced on the diagonal into $^1/_2$-inch slices
- 3 tablespoons olive oil

Preheat the oven to 300°. In a small bowl, stir together the scallions, blue cheese, and tarragon. Brush the baguette slices with olive oil. Place the slices on a sheet pan and bake until they are crunchy and golden brown, 8 to 10 minutes.

Remove the slices from the oven and preheat the broiler. Spread each baguette slice with 2 teaspoons of the cheese mixture and broil until the cheese is bubbly and melted, about 3 minutes.

basil purée

Makes about 1 cup

Try all of the purées on top of the Bistro Potato Soup (page 55). They're equally delicious on top of the chowders. I also use the basil purée on top of turkey, portobello, and roasted pepper sandwiches.

- 1 cup packed fresh basil leaves
- 1 clove garlic
- 1 cup extra-virgin olive oil

Place all the ingredients in the bowl of a food processor. Process until smooth. Keep refrigerated until ready to use.

Variations

When using a stronger herb, such as rosemary or tarragon, I suggest cutting the herb amount in half and adding spinach leaves to make up the other half.

Rosemary Purée: $^1/_2$ cup rosemary, $^1/_2$ cup fresh spinach leaves, and 1 cup extra-virgin olive oil.

Tarragon Purée: $^1/_2$ cup tarragon, $^1/_2$ cup fresh spinach leaves, and 1 cup extra-virgin olive oil.

Cilantro Purée: $^1/_2$ cup cilantro, $^1/_2$ cup fresh spinach leaves, and 1 cup extra-virgin olive oil.

Watercress Purée: 1 cup packed watercress leaves and 1 cup extra-virgin olive oil.

tapenade

Makes about 1/2 cup

In the South of France, black olive tapenade is called "black butter" because it's spread on anything and everything. At the Bistro, we treat it the same way, putting it on potato soup, burgers, and even ratatouille sandwiches.

> 1/2 cup pitted cured black olives
>
> 2 cloves garlic
>
> 1/2 teaspoon capers
>
> 1 oil- or salt-packed anchovy fillet, drained
>
> 1 teaspoon freshly squeezed lemon juice
>
> 2 tablespoons extra-virgin olive oil

In the bowl of a food processor, combine the olives, garlic, capers, anchovy, and lemon juice, and process until smooth. With the machine running, slowly add the olive oil through the feeder tube and process until smooth. Refrigerate until ready to use.

cucumber-yogurt sauce

Makes 2 cups

We use this sauce mostly for Middle Eastern-influenced dishes, such as the Yellow Tomato and Garbanzo Bean Soup (page 52). It would also be a nice addition to the Lamb Sandwich (page 84).

> 1 cup plain yogurt
>
> 2 cloves garlic, chopped
>
> 1 small cucumber, shredded

> 1 teaspoon toasted, ground cumin (page 120)
>
> Salt
>
> Freshly ground black pepper

In a small bowl, combine the yogurt, garlic, cucumber, and cumin, and mix well. Season with salt and pepper. Chill until ready to use.

rouille

Makes about 1 cup

A rouille is the traditional sauce drizzled over bouillabaisse, but it's also a snazzy addition to the Three-Cheese Sandwich (page 103).

> 1/4 cup toasted bread crumbs (page 120)
>
> 1 egg
>
> 1/2 red bell pepper, roasted, peeled and seeded (page 118)
>
> 2 cloves garlic
>
> 1/4 cup chopped basil
>
> 1/2 cup extra-virgin olive oil
>
> 1 teaspoon chile sauce
>
> Juice of 1 lemon
>
> 1 teaspoon capers
>
> 1 teaspoon salt

Place the bread crumbs in the bowl of a food processor. Add the egg and pepper, and purée until smooth. Add the garlic and basil, and process until smooth. With the machine running, add the olive oil through the feed tube. Process until emulsified. Add the chile sauce, lemon juice, capers, and salt, and process until smooth. Refrigerate until ready to use.

BISTRO Soups

Black Bean Soup with Chocolate / 18

Chanterelle Velvet with Rosemary
Croutons / 19

Bouillabaisse / 21

Chicken with Noodles and Herbs and
Tarragon Purée/ 22

Lamb Stew with Wild Mushrooms
and Figs / 23

Hot-and-Sour Soup with
Five-Spice Chicken / 25

Lima Bean Soup with Saffron / 27

Mark's Gumbo / 29

Mediterranean Vegetable Soup / 31

Red Bell Pepper Soup with
Corn Spoon Bread / 33

Red Seafood Chowder / 35

Chicken and Blue Cheese Dumplings / 37

Spicy Peanut Soup with Curry and
Vegetables / 39

Shellfish Bisque / 40

Savory Tomato and Tomatillo Soup with
Chiles and Chicken Meatballs / 44

Sweet Summer Corn Soup with
Red Bell Pepper and Basil Purées / 47

White Bean Soup with Sundried Tomatoes
and Pancetta / 48

Wild Mushroom Soup with
Corn and Crab / 49

Fall Squash Soup with Chorizo and
Spicy Cinnamon Croutons / 51

Yellow Tomato and Garbanzo Bean Soup
with Cucumber-Yogurt Sauce / 52

Sweet Potato and
Carmelized Onion Soup / 53

Bistro Potato Soup / 55

Split Pea Soup with Tasso Ham and
Andouille Sausage / 56

Bistro Chowder / 57

Onion Soup with Scallion-Roquefort
Croustades / 58

black bean soup
WITH CHOCOLATE

Serves 6 to 8

Folding chocolate into soup may seem strange, but the bit of sweetness offsets the spicy flavors of this soup and gives it a beautiful sheen. Try adding sautéed chorizo, linguiça, or another spicy sausage, or make the soup vegetarian by leaving out the ham hock.

1¹/₂ pounds dried black beans

1 smoked ham hock

3 bay leaves

8 to 10 cups water

2 tablespoons olive oil

1 large onion, diced

2 jalapeño peppers, seeded and
   finely diced

6 cloves garlic, minced

¹/₂ teaspoon ground cinnamon

2 tablespoons chile powder

2 tablespoons cumin

Zest of 1 orange

1 cup dry red wine

1 cup bittersweet chocolate, chopped

2 teaspoons cayenne sauce

Salt

Freshly ground black pepper

Crème fraîche, for garnish (page 122)

Cilantro purée, for garnish (page 14)

Mango relish or tomato relish, for
   garnish (pages 95 and 92)

In a large stockpot over medium-high heat, combine the beans, ham hock, bay leaves, and 8 cups of water. Bring the mixture to a boil. Reduce the heat and let the soup simmer for 2¹/₂ to 3 hours, or until the beans are tender (add additional water if necessary). Remove the bay leaves and ham hock. Set the ham aside to cool, then pull the meat off the bones and cut into bite-sized pieces. Set aside.

About 30 minutes before the beans are tender, heat the oil in a large skillet over medium-high heat until hot. Sauté the onion, jalapeños, and garlic until the onion is tender, 5 to 8 minutes. Add the cinnamon, chile powder, cumin, orange zest, and red wine, and cook over high heat until reduced by half, about 5 minutes. Add the chocolate and stir until melted. Add the ham and stir in.

Stir the onion mixture into the simmering bean mixture and simmer 20 minutes longer. Adjust thickness of the soup with more water. Add the cayenne sauce and season to taste with salt and pepper.

To serve, ladle the soup into bowls and garnish with crème fraîche, cilantro purée, and mango relish or tomato relish.

chanterelle *velvet*

WITH ROSEMARY CROUTONS

Serves 6 to 8

*We like to make this soup in the fall, during
the peak of the chanterelle season, as a cele-
bration of the harvest and autumn's riches.
To turn it into a heartier soup, stir in pieces
of roasted chicken.*

$^1/_2$ **cup butter**

$^1/_2$ **cup rice flour**

$^1/_4$ **cup flour**

1 gallon chicken stock (page 8)

3 tablespoons olive oil

2 pounds chanterelles

1 onion, diced

4 shallots, chopped

4 cloves garlic, minced

1 cup marsala or dry sherry

4 cups whipping cream

2 tablespoons sherry vinegar

1 tablespoon Worcestershire sauce

Salt

Freshly ground black pepper

**Rosemary croutons, for garnish
    (page 13)**

To make a roux, melt the butter in a small
saucepan over medium heat, stir in the flours,
and cook, stirring continuously, until the
roux is golden brown and fragrant, about
5 minutes. Set aside to cool.

In a large stockpot over high heat, bring
the chicken stock to a boil. Whisk in the roux
and cook until reduced by one-third.

Meanwhile, heat the olive oil in a large
sauté pan over high heat until hot. Add the
chanterelles, onion, shallots, and garlic, and
cook 5 to 8 minutes. Add the marsala and
reduce over high heat until about $^1/_2$ cup of
liquid remains.

In a food processor or blender, purée the
vegetable mixture. Then whisk it into the
stock. Whisk in the cream, vinegar, and
Worcestershire sauce, and season to taste with
salt and pepper.

To serve, ladle the soup into large bowls
and garnish with the croutons.

bouillabaisse

Serves 6 to 8

This is a popular French classic, simplified for your kitchen. At the Bistro, we throw in the freshest Northwest seafood. Use the very best seasonal seafood you can find and serve the soup with a robust, dry red wine and a crusty loaf of French bread.

2 tablespoons olive oil

3 leeks, white parts only, rinsed well and
 sliced crosswise

1 bulb fennel, julienned, the greens
 reserved for garnish

3 cloves garlic, minced

Pinch of saffron threads

1 cup dry white wine

Zest of 1 orange

8 cups fish or seafood stock (page 12)

1 pound halibut or other firm white fish

1 pound sea scallops

1 pound mussels or hard-shell
 butter clams

1 pound prawns, peeled and deveined

2 or 3 vine-ripened tomatoes, seeded
 and chopped (page 118)

1 teaspoon chopped fresh thyme

1 teaspoon chopped fresh marjoram

1 tablespoon Pernod or anisette

Salt

Freshly ground black pepper

Rouille, for garnish (page 15)

Crostini, for garnish (page 13)

Heat the olive oil in a large stockpot over medium-high heat until hot. Sauté the leeks, fennel, garlic, and saffron threads until fragrant, 2 to 3 minutes. Add the wine and orange zest, and cook over high heat until reduced by half, about 5 minutes, and then add the stock. When the stock begins to boil, reduce the heat and simmer for 8 to 10 minutes. Add the halibut and scallops, cover the pot with the lid, and cook until the fish is firm and opaque, about 2 minutes. Add the mussels and prawns. Cover the pot with the lid, and cook until the mussels open and the prawns turn pink, 1 to 2 minutes. Stir in the tomatoes, herbs, and liqueur, and cook until the tomatoes are just heated through, about 2 minutes. Season to taste with salt and pepper.

To serve, ladle the bouillabaisse into large, shallow bowls and garnish with rouille and crostini.

chicken with noodles *and herbs*

AND TARRAGON PURÉE

Serves 6 to 8

This is our twist on the ultimate comfort soup. For a variation, omit the noodles and serve the soup with corn spoon bread (page 33).

1 (3- to 4-pound) chicken

8 cups chicken stock (page 8)

2 tablespoons olive oil

3 onions, julienned

3 carrots, peeled and julienned

3 stalks celery, cut into $1/4$-inch slices

6 cloves garlic, minced

1 cup dry white wine

Salt

Freshly ground pepper

$1/2$ pound noodles or pasta, such as fettuccine or fresh ravioli

Tarragon purée, for garnish (page 14)

In a large stockpot over medium-high heat, bring the chicken and stock to a boil. Reduce the heat to low and simmer until the chicken is cooked through, about 1 hour. Remove the chicken from the broth; keep the broth simmering over low heat. Pull the meat from the bones, cut it into bite-sized pieces, and set aside.

Heat the olive oil in a large sauté pan over medium-high heat until hot. Add the onions, carrots, celery, and garlic, and cook until tender and fragrant, 5 to 8 minutes. Add the wine and cook over high heat until reduced by half.

Add the noodles to the simmering broth and cook until al dente. Stir in the vegetable mixture and season to taste with salt and pepper.

To serve, ladle the soup into bowls and garnish with the chicken and tarragon purée.

lamb stew

WITH WILD MUSHROOMS AND FIGS

Serves 6 to 8

During the holidays, we had a dine-around dinner with each course served at a different house. Mark created this earthy, intensely flavored dish specifically for that night. The figs add a touch of sweetness and soak up the rich tones of the lamb and port.

- 3 to 4 pounds lamb stew meat, cut into 1-inch cubes
- 2 cups flour
- 1/4 cup olive oil
- 1 pound pancetta, diced
- 1 large onion, diced
- 1 pound assorted wild mushrooms, sliced
- 3 cloves garlic, minced
- 1/4 cup balsamic vinegar
- 1 cup port
- 2 cups Syrah or other medium- or full-bodied red wine
- 2 cups beef stock (page 9)
- 1 pound young carrots, peeled and left whole
- 1 pound baby red potatoes, quartered
- 1 pound dried Calimyrna or Mission figs, halved and stemmed
- 1 tablespoon chopped fresh rosemary
- Salt
- Freshly ground black pepper

Preheat the oven to 325°. Dredge the lamb in the flour.

Heat the oil in a large ovenproof stockpot over medium-high heat until hot. Add the pancetta and cook until it is crispy. Remove the pancetta from the pot and set aside.

Heat the pancetta fat over high heat until lightly smoking. Add the lamb and sear well on all sides until brown, about 5 minutes total. Remove the lamb from the pot and set aside.

Add the onion, mushrooms, and garlic, and sauté until the onions are tender, 4 to 5 minutes. Add the vinegar, port, and red wine, and cook over high heat until reduced by one-half. Add the stock and the lamb, bring to a boil, and cover the pot with a lid. Braise the stew in the oven for 1 hour.

Remove the stew from the oven and add the carrots, potatoes, figs, and rosemary. Cover the pot and return it to the oven to braise for an additional 30 minutes, or until the vegetables are tender. Season to taste with salt and pepper.

To serve, ladle the soup into bowls and top with the pancetta.

hot-and-sour soup

WITH FIVE-SPICE CHICKEN

Serves 6 to 8

Here in Portland we have a big Asian community, and hot-and-sour soup is a very popular dish. Our version is easy to make and can be modified to be as simple or elaborate as you like. Tofu and miso broth can be substituted for the chicken and stock.

- 1/4 cup five-spice marinade
  (page 122)
- 4 boneless chicken breasts
- 1/4 cup peanut oil or olive oil
- 8 cups chicken stock (page 8)
- 2 onions, julienned
- 1/4 cup peeled, julienned ginger root
- 6 cloves garlic, minced
- 1 tablespoon dark sesame oil
- 1 cup dry sherry or mirin
- 1 cup soy sauce
- 1/2 cup tamarind pulp
- 1 tablespoon sambal oelek or
  2 teaspoons dried chile flakes
- 3 carrots, peeled and julienned
- 1/2 pound shiitake mushrooms, sliced
- 1 pound snow peas
- 1 bunch bok choy, sliced on the diagonal
- 2 or 3 scallions, sliced on the diagonal
- 1 cup freshly squeezed lime juice
- 1/2 cup rice wine vinegar
- 1/4 cup arrowroot powder or cornstarch
- 1/4 cup water
- 6 to 8 sprigs cilantro, for garnish
- 4 ounces radish sprouts, for garnish
- 6 to 8 whole star anise, for garnish

Coat the chicken breasts with the marinade and refrigerate for 1 hour.

Heat 2 tablespoons of the oil in a large sauté pan over high heat until smoking hot. Add the chicken breasts and sear for about 3 minutes per side, or until cooked through. Slice the breasts into 1/2-inch slices. Set aside and keep warm.

In a large stockpot over medium-high heat, bring the stock to a boil. Reduce the heat to low and simmer.

Meanwhile, heat the remaining 2 tablespoons of oil in a wok or large sauté pan over high heat until smoking hot. Sauté the onions, ginger root, garlic, and sesame oil until the mixture is fragrant and the onions are tender, 3 to 4 minutes. Add the sherry, soy sauce, tamarind pulp, and sambal, and cook for 2 minutes, then add the mixture to the simmering stock. Add the carrots, shiitake mushrooms, snow peas, bok choy,

continued from page 25

and scallions, and simmer until the bok choy is crisp-tender, about 2 minutes. Stir in the lime juice and vinegar. In a small bowl, stir together the arrowroot powder or cornstarch and water, and slowly whisk it into the soup to thicken. Simmer for another 2 minutes.

To serve, ladle the soup into bowls and garnish with sliced chicken, cilantro sprigs, radish sprouts, and star anise.

lima bean soup *with saffron*

Serves 6 to 8

One day I was looking forward to having a bowl of Mark's soup of the day—until he told me it was lima bean soup. He coaxed me into tasting it, and I was won over. Try adding hot Italian sausage for a spicy alternative, or make it with fish stock and garnish with shrimp.

1 pound dried lima beans, sorted and
   rinsed
2 tablespoons olive oil
2 onions, cut into small dice
6 cloves garlic, minced
1 cup dry white wine
2 teaspoons saffron threads
6 cups chicken stock (page 8)
1 red bell pepper, roasted, peeled,
   seeded, and julienned (page 118)
1 teaspoon cayenne sauce
1 tablespoon Pernod or anisette
Salt
Freshly ground black pepper
2 tablespoons chopped fresh Italian
   parsley, for garnish
Tomato relish or fennel jam, for garnish
   (pages 92 and 76)

Place the beans in a large stockpot, cover with cold water, and soak 3 hours or overnight.

Bring the beans and soaking water to a boil over medium-high heat. Partially cover the pot, decrease the heat to low, and simmer until tender, about 45 minutes, adding more water if needed. Drain the beans and set aside.

Heat the olive oil in a stockpot over medium-high heat. Sauté the onions and garlic until fragrant and tender. Add the wine and saffron, and reduce over high heat by one-half. Add the stock and bell peppers, bring to a boil, decrease the heat, and simmer 10 to 15 minutes. Pour the beans into the stock mixture and simmer 25 to 30 minutes, or until the flavors are well blended. Stir in the cayenne sauce and liqueur, and season to taste with salt and pepper.

To serve, ladle the soup into bowls and garnish with parsley and tomato relish or fennel jam.

mark's gumbo

Serves 6 to 8

Mark spent a summer in New Orleans and fell in love with the regional flavors. This dish captures the essence of the Big Easy while showcasing the Northwest's bounty. We always call our good friends Oz and Robert when gumbo is coming up on the menu so they won't miss out on their favorite dish.

1 cup rendered bacon or duck fat

1¹/₂ cups flour

1 teaspoon cayenne pepper

1 gallon seafood, chicken, or beef stock,
    or a combination of these stocks
    (pages 8–12)

2 onions, diced

1 jalapeño pepper, minced

1 red bell pepper, cut into large dice

1 green bell pepper, cut into large dice

1 yellow bell pepper, cut into large dice

3 cloves garlic, minced

2 pounds andouille sausage, cut into
    ¹/₄-inch discs

1 pound tasso ham, chopped

2 pounds okra, sliced

1 teaspoon paprika

1 teaspoon chile powder

1 teaspoon ground cumin

1 cup dry red wine

1 (16-ounce) can tomato purée

2 teaspoons cayenne sauce, or to taste

2 teaspoons Worcestershire sauce

1 teaspoon filé powder

1 pound prawns, peeled and deveined

1 pound scallops

1 pound boneless chicken or
    duck breast, diced

Salt

Freshly ground black pepper

4 cups cooked white rice (page 120)

Preheat the oven to 350°. To make a roux, melt the rendered fat in a large sauté pan over medium-high heat. Add the flour and cayenne pepper, and cook, stirring continuously, until the ingredients are well blended. Transfer to a baking pan and bake, stirring every 20 to 30 minutes, for 1¹/₂ to 2 hours, or until deep brown.

    Bring the stock to a boil in a large stockpot over medium-high heat, whisk in the roux, and cook over high heat until reduced by one-half.

    Meanwhile, in a large sauté pan over medium-high heat, combine the onions, peppers, garlic, andouille sausage, tasso ham, and okra. Cover the pan with a lid and cook until the vegetables are tender and fragrant, 5 to 8 minutes. Add the paprika, chile powder, cumin, and red wine, and cook over high heat

continued from page 29

until reduced by one-half, about 5 minutes. Add the tomato purée, bring to a boil, reduce the heat to low, and simmer 5 to 10 minutes, or until the flavors are well blended. Stir the vegetable mixture into the stock. Add the cayenne sauce, Worcestershire sauce, and filé powder. Add the prawns, scallops, and chicken, and simmer until the prawns turn pink, the scallops are opaque, and the chicken is just cooked. Adjust the thickness of the gumbo with additional stock or water, if necessary, and season to taste with salt and pepper. Serve hot over white rice, and pass around a bottle of Louisiana-style hot sauce.

mediterranean vegetable soup

Serves 6 to 8

Take advantage of the seasonal vegetables in your area and make a pot of this ultimate vegetable soup. After you chop the vegetables, it comes together in a snap.

3 tablespoons olive oil

1 large onion, diced

2 stalks celery, cut into small dice

2 carrots, peeled and diced

2 eggplants, diced

1 bulb fennel, diced

6 cloves garlic, minced

1 teaspoon saffron threads

Zest of 1 orange

2 tablespoons orange juice concentrate

1 cup dry white wine

1 (16-ounce) can garbanzo beans, undrained

1 (28-ounce) can chopped tomatoes in juice

1 (28-ounce) can tomato purée

4 cups chicken or vegetable stock (pages 8 and 9)

2 teaspoons chopped fresh rosemary

2 teaspoons chopped fresh thyme

2 teaspoons chopped fresh parsley

2 tablespoons balsamic vinegar

Salt

Freshly ground black pepper

Tapenade (page 15)

Fennel jam, for garnish (page 76)

Heat the olive oil in a large stockpot over medium heat until hot. Add the onion, celery, carrots, eggplant, and fennel. Turn the heat to medium-low and cook until the fennel is tender, 5 to 8 minutes.

Increase the heat to medium, add the garlic, saffron, orange zest, and juice concentrate, and cook until reduced by one-half, about 5 minutes. Add the wine and reduce over high heat until $1/2$ cup liquid remains, about 5 minutes. Add the garbanzo beans, tomatoes, tomato purée, stock, and herbs.

Bring the soup to a boil, reduce the heat, and simmer 25 to 30 minutes, or until the flavors are well blended. Stir in the balsamic vinegar and season to taste with salt and pepper.

To serve, ladle the soup into bowls and garnish with the tapenade and fennel jam.

red bell pepper soup

WITH CORN SPOON BREAD

Serves 6 to 8

To develop the spoon bread recipe, Mark spent an afternoon in the vintage section of a cookbook store in search of tried-and-true methods for making this old-fashioned dish. In addition to this soup, the spoon bread also goes well with grilled fish or a roasted chicken.

corn spoon bread

2 cups milk

2 cups chicken stock (page 8) or water

1^1/$_2$ cups finely ground cornmeal

Kernels from 4 ears fresh corn (about 3 cups)

6 eggs, separated

1 teaspoon cayenne sauce

2 cloves garlic, minced

2 teaspoons salt

1 teaspoon freshly ground black pepper

1 cup grated Cheddar

^{1}/$_4$ cup flour

1 teaspoon baking powder

2 tablespoons olive oil

1 large onion, diced

8 to 10 red bell peppers, seeded and chopped

6 cloves garlic, minced

1 cup dry white wine

1 (28-ounce) can chopped tomatoes in purée

8 cups chicken stock (page 8)

2 teaspoons Worcestershire sauce

2 teaspoons cayenne sauce

1 tablespoon rice wine vinegar

To prepare the spoon bread, preheat the oven to 375°. In a large saucepan over medium-high heat, bring the milk and stock to a boil. Reduce the heat to low, slowly whisk in the cornmeal, and cook, whisking often, until smooth and creamy, about 5 minutes. Stir in the corn and set aside to cool.

In a small bowl, whisk together the egg yolks, cayenne sauce, garlic, salt, and pepper. Add the egg yolk mixture and cheese to the cornmeal mixture, stirring well. Sift together the flour and baking powder, and stir it into the batter. Whip the egg whites until soft peaks form and fold them into the batter. Pour the batter into a greased 9 x 13-inch baking pan and bake 45 minutes to 1 hour, or until a toothpick comes out clean when inserted in the center. Set aside.

To prepare the soup, heat the olive oil in a large stockpot over medium-high heat until

continued from page 33

hot. Sauté the onion, peppers, and garlic until tender, about 5 minutes. Add the wine and cook over high heat until reduced by one-half. Add the tomatoes and chicken stock, and bring the mixture to a boil over medium-high heat. Reduce the heat to low and simmer 25 to 30 minutes.

Purée the soup in batches in a food processor or blender, strain back into a clean pot over medium-high heat, and cook 5 minutes. Stir in the Worcestershire sauce, cayenne sauce, and vinegar.

To serve, ladle the soup into bowls and top with a piece of spoon bread.

red seafood chowder

Serves 6 to 8

This is a twist on Manhattan chowder. Mark makes it zestier by adding horseradish and cayenne sauce.

6 cups fish stock (page 12) or
    clam juice

1 (28-ounce) can chopped tomatoes in
    purée

4 red potatoes, peeled and diced

2 tablespoons olive oil

2 onions, chopped

1 small celeriac, peeled and diced

1 bulb fennel, diced

2 carrots, peeled and diced

6 cloves garlic, minced

1 cup dry white wine

2 pounds fresh seafood, such as
    baby scallops, crabmeat, clams, cod,
    or shrimp

1 tablespoon prepared horseradish

Juice and zest of 1 lemon

1 tablespoon Worcestershire sauce

1 tablespoon cayenne sauce

Salt

Freshly ground black pepper

2 tablespoons chopped fresh Italian
    parsley, for garnish

In a large stockpot over medium-high heat, bring the fish stock, tomatoes, and potatoes to a boil. Reduce the heat to low and simmer 8 to 10 minutes, until the potatoes are tender. Set aside.

Heat the olive oil in a large saucepan over medium-high heat until hot. Add the onions, celeriac, fennel, carrots, and garlic, cover the pan with a lid, decrease the heat to medium-low, and cook 8 to 10 minutes, or until tender. Add the wine and reduce over high heat until $1/4$ cup liquid remains, about 5 minutes. Heat the tomato mixture over medium-high heat until boiling. Add the vegetable mixture and the seafood, reduce the heat to low, and simmer just until the fish is cooked, 3 to 4 minutes. Stir in the horseradish, lemon juice and zest, Worcestershire sauce, and cayenne sauce, and season to taste with salt and pepper.

To serve, ladle into bowls and garnish with parsley.

chicken and *blue cheese* dumplings

Serves 6 to 8

Mark invented this dish when he was making traditional chicken and dumplings and had a craving for blue cheese at the same time. The savory dumplings and the juicy chicken are perfect with an Oregon Pinot Noir.

2 cups flour

2 teaspoons salt

2 teaspoons freshly ground black pepper

1 (4- to 5-pound) chicken, cut into
    pieces

$^1/_4$ cup olive oil

1 large onion, diced

6 cloves garlic, minced

2 cups dry white wine or dry sherry

6 cups chicken stock (page 8)

4 to 6 medium-sized red potatoes, cut
    into large dice

3 carrots, peeled, halved lengthwise, and
    sliced into $^1/_4$-inch pieces

3 stalks celery, cut into $^1/_4$-inch dice

2 red bell peppers, roasted, peeled,
    seeded, and diced (page 118)

$^1/_2$ pound morels or shiitakes, sliced

2 zucchini, halved lengthwise and sliced
    into $^1/_4$-inch pieces

Sprigs of rosemary, for garnish

blue cheese dumplings

2 cups flour

4 teaspoons baking powder

1 teaspoon salt

1 cup milk

$^1/_4$ cup vegetable oil

1 tablespoon chopped fresh rosemary,
    oregano, thyme, parsley, or other
    fresh herb

$1^1/_2$ cups crumbled blue cheese

In a large, shallow bowl, combine the flour, salt, and pepper. Dredge the chicken pieces in the flour mixture and set aside.

Preheat the oven to 350°. Heat the oil in a large, ovenproof stockpot over medium-high heat until smoking hot. Add as many chicken pieces as will fit in the pan without over-crowding and sear them on both sides until brown, about 2 minutes per side. Transfer the chicken to a plate and set aside. Repeat with the remaining pieces. Add the onion and garlic to the pot, and sauté until tender and fragrant, about 3 minutes. Add the wine and cook over high heat until reduced by one-half. Add the stock, bring it to a boil, and add the chicken, making sure the stock covers each piece. Cover the pot and braise in the oven 35 to 40 minutes, or until the chicken is

continued from page 37

tender when pierced with a fork. Add the potatoes, carrots, celery, and roasted bell peppers. Cover with a lid and braise in the oven 25 minutes longer, or until the potatoes and carrots are tender.

Meanwhile, make the dumplings. Sift together the flour, baking powder, and salt. In a large bowl, combine the milk, vegetable oil, herbs, and blue cheese. Gradually add the flour mixture, stirring just until the dough is moist and comes together (overmixing results in tough dumplings).

Stir the mushrooms and zucchini into the bubbling stew. Drop tablespoons of dough onto the surface of the stew. Cover the pan, return it to the oven, and cook for another 10 to 15 minutes, or until a knife inserted in the dumplings comes out clean. Garnish with sprigs of rosemary and serve immediately.

spicy peanut soup
WITH CURRY AND VEGETABLES

Serves 6 to 8

Bistro regulars Bob and Mary request any dish with curry, and this is one of their favorites. You can easily change this recipe by adding raw shrimp or diced pork near the end of the cooking process, simmering it until it is cooked through.

2 tablespoons olive oil

2 teaspoons sesame oil

2 onions, diced

3 cloves garlic, chopped

1 tablespoon sambal oelek or
    chile sauce

1 tablespoon instant sour paste or
    tamarind pulp

2 tablespoons curry powder

$1/2$ teaspoon ground cumin

$1/2$ teaspoon ground coriander seeds

1 cup mirin or dry sherry

$1/2$ cup soy sauce

2 cups creamy peanut butter

2 (14-ounce) cans coconut milk

$1/4$ cup palm sugar or honey

8 cups vegetable stock (page 9) or
    miso broth

2 cups heavy whipping cream

2 tablespoons rice wine vinegar

Salt

Freshly ground black pepper

1 cup broccoli florets, blanched,
    for garnish (page 120)

6 baby bok choy, blanched, for garnish
    (page 120)

$1/4$ cup chopped fresh cilantro,
    for garnish

$1/2$ cup chopped roasted peanuts,
    for garnish

Balinese sambal, for garnish (page 72)

Heat the olive oil and sesame oil in a large stockpot over medium-high heat until hot. Sauté the onions, garlic, sambal oelek, instant sour paste, curry powder, cumin, and coriander until fragrant and the onions are tender, about 5 minutes. Whisk in the mirin, soy sauce, peanut butter, coconut milk, and palm sugar. Add the stock and bring to a boil. Reduce the heat to low and simmer 30 minutes.

Stir in the cream and vinegar. Season to taste with salt and pepper, and adjust the flavor with additional sambal oelek, if desired.

To serve, ladle the soup into soup bowls and garnish with the blanched vegetables, cilantro, peanuts, and Balinese sambal.

shellfish bisque

Serves 6 to 8

For a memorable dinner party, make this elegant soup the focus and serve it with a crisp Pinot Gris. At the Bistro, Mark likes to give the recipe an Asian twist by adding ginger root and lemongrass.

1 pound medium prawns, shelled and
    deveined, shells reserved

1 pound crabmeat, shells reserved

1 pound crayfish, cooked and cleaned,
    shells reserved (page 119)

2 (8- to 10-ounce) cooked lobster tails,
    shelled, shells reserved and meat cut
    into bite-sized pieces (page 119)

$^1/_2$ cup butter

$^1/_2$ cup flour

1 gallon fish stock (page 12)

2 tablespoons olive oil

2 onions, diced

2 stalks celery, chopped

2 carrots, peeled and diced

1 bulb fennel, chopped

6 cloves garlic, minced

2 teaspoons freshly ground black pepper

1 tablespoon paprika

2 tablespoons fennel seeds

3 tablespoons tomato paste

1 cup dry white wine or dry sherry

$^1/_4$ cup brandy

4 cups whipping cream

1 tablespoon Worcestershire sauce

1 tablespoon cayenne sauce

1 tablespoon Pernod or other licorice-
    flavored liqueur

Salt

White pepper

Preheat the oven to 350°. Place the reserved shells on a sheet pan and roast 20 minutes. Remove the shells from the oven and allow them to cool. Grind the cooled shells in small batches in a food processor. Set aside.

To make a roux, melt the butter in a medium sauté pan until hot. Stir in the flour and cook, stirring continuously, until it smells nutty and is golden brown, about 20 minutes. Set aside to cool.

Bring the fish stock to a boil in a large stockpot over high heat. Whisk in the roux, decrease the heat to low, and simmer until the liquid is thickened and reduced by one third, about 45 minutes.

Meanwhile, heat the olive oil in another large stockpot over medium heat until hot. Add the onions, celery, carrots, fennel, garlic, and shells, and sauté 5 minutes. Add the peppercorns, paprika, fennel seeds, tomato paste, wine, and brandy, and cook over high heat until the liquid is reduced by one-half.

Pour in the thickened stock and simmer over low heat until reduced by one-half, about 45 minutes.

Strain the stock mixture through a fine sieve into a clean pot over medium-high heat. Whisk in the cream and bring to a boil. Add the seafood and simmer until the prawns are pink. Add the Worcestershire sauce, cayenne sauce, and liqueur, and season to taste with salt and white pepper. Serve hot.

savory tomato *and* tomatillo soup
WITH CHILES AND CHICKEN MEATBALLS

Serves 6 to 8

If you prefer, you can bake the meatballs on a sheet pan instead of poaching them in the soup. Either way, they'll taste great with the tangy tomatillos and a splash of lime.

chicken meatballs

1¹/₂ pounds ground chicken

1 cup fresh bread crumbs

1 clove garlic, minced

¹/₂ teaspoon ground cumin

1 teaspoon chile powder

2 teaspoons salt

1 teaspoon freshly ground black pepper

¹/₂ cup cooked white rice (page 120)

1 egg, beaten

Zest of 1 lime, finely chopped

1 tablespoon chopped fresh cilantro

soup

2 tablespoons olive oil

1 medium onion, cut into small dice

2 carrots, peeled and cut into small dice

2 stalks celery, diced

6 cloves garlic, minced

1 pound fresh tomatillos, husks removed, sliced

6 to 8 assorted chile peppers, such as Anaheim, serrano, jalapeño, or red bell peppers, julienned

1 cup dry white wine

2 teaspoons ground cumin

1 teaspoon ground coriander

2 teaspoons chile powder

1 (28-ounce) can chopped tomatoes in purée

8 cups chicken stock (page 8)

Zest and juice of 2 limes

1 tablespoon rice wine vinegar

1 tablespoon cayenne sauce, or to taste

Salt

Freshly ground black pepper

6 to 8 sprigs fresh cilantro, chopped, for garnish

Crème fraîche, for garnish (page 122)

To make the meatballs, in a large bowl, combine all of the meatball ingredients until well mixed. With your hands, form the mixture into about 24 meatballs. Set aside.

To make the soup, preheat the oven to 350°. Heat the olive oil in a large ovenproof stockpot or Dutch oven over medium-high heat until hot. Add the onion, carrots, celery, garlic, tomatillos, and chile peppers, and cook until the carrots are tender and fragrant, 5 to 8 minutes. Add the wine, cumin, coriander, chile powder, tomatoes, and stock, and bring to a boil. Add the meat-balls, cover the pot with a lid, and braise in the oven until the meatballs are done, 35 to 45 minutes.

Remove the soup from the oven and skim off any fat that has formed on the surface. Stir in the lime juice, vinegar, and cayenne sauce, and season to taste with salt and pepper.

To serve, ladle the soup into large, shallow bowls and garnish with cilantro, reserved lime zest, and crème fraîche. Pass around a bottle of cayenne sauce.

sweet summer corn soup

WITH RED BELL PEPPER AND BASIL PURÉES

Serves 6 to 8

Mark makes this soup only during the summer, when fresh, sweet corn is at its peak. As an option, garnish the soup with cooked lobster or crab.

8 cups chicken, fish, or seafood stock
(pages 8–12)
1 tablespoon olive oil
1 large onion, diced
6 cloves garlic, minced
Kernels cut from 12 ears fresh corn
(about 10 cups)
1 cup dry white wine
2 cups heavy whipping cream
2 teaspoons cayenne sauce, or to taste
2 teaspoons Worcestershire sauce
Salt
Freshly ground black pepper
Roasted red bell pepper purée, for
garnish (page 118)
Basil purée, for garnish (page 14)
6 to 8 sprigs watercress, for garnish
Cooked lobster or crab, for garnish,
optional (page 119)

In a large stockpot over medium-high heat, bring the stock to a boil. Decrease the heat to low and simmer.

Meanwhile, heat the olive oil in another large stockpot over medium-high heat until hot. Add the onion, garlic, and half of the corn, and sauté until the onion is tender, about 5 minutes. Add the wine and cook over high heat until reduced by one-half. Pour in half of the hot stock and simmer over low heat, about 5 minutes.

Strain the mixture into the remaining stock. Purée the solids in a blender or food processor, strain again, and add to the stock mixture. Reduce the soup by one-half over medium-high heat, then stir in the remaining corn, the cream, cayenne sauce, and Worcestershire sauce. Season to taste with salt and pepper.

To serve, ladle the soup into bowls and drizzle with the bell pepper and basil purées. Garnish with watercress and seafood.

white bean soup

WITH SUNDRIED TOMATOES AND PANCETTA

Serves 6 to 8

I don't want to dwell on Portland's damp weather, but when it rains, the Bistro is extra cozy, the perfect atmosphere for bean soup. This soup, with its bright flavors of sundried tomatoes and fennel, will cure you of the winter blues.

1 pound dried cannellini, flageolet,
    great Northern, or other white beans,
    sorted and rinsed

12 cups chicken stock (page 8)

2 bay leaves

2 tablespoons olive oil

1 pound pancetta or pepper bacon, diced

2 medium onions, diced

1 bulb fennel, diced

6 cloves garlic, minced

1 cup dry white wine

1 cup oil-packed sundried tomatoes,
    drained and julienned

1 teaspoon chopped fresh thyme

2 tablespoons Worcestershire sauce

1 tablespoon rice wine vinegar

Salt

Freshly ground black pepper

Tarragon purée or fennel jam,
    for garnish (pages 14 and 76)

Place the beans in a large bowl. Cover with cold water and let them soak 3 to 4 hours. Drain and rinse.

In a large stockpot over medium-high heat, combine the beans, stock, and bay leaves. Bring to a boil, decrease the heat, and simmer until the beans are tender, $1^1/2$ to 2 hours, adding more stock or water if necessary.

Meanwhile, heat the olive oil in a large sauté pan over medium-high heat until hot. Add the pancetta and cook until crispy, but not too brown. Add the onions, fennel, and garlic, and sauté until the mixture is fragrant and the onions are tender, about 5 minutes. Add the white wine and sundried tomatoes, and cook over high heat until the liquid is reduced by one-half. Stir the vegetable mixture into the beans and bring to a boil over medium-high heat. Reduce the heat to low, and simmer 25 to 30 minutes.

Stir in the thyme, Worcestershire sauce, and vinegar, and season to taste with salt and pepper. Adjust the consistency of the soup with more stock or water, if needed.

To serve, ladle soup into soup bowls and garnish with tarragon purée or fennel jam.

wild mushroom soup

WITH CORN AND CRAB

Serves 6 to 8

A group of our closest friends gathered these ingredients out in the wine country one fall afternoon. We made this soup when we returned home and were surprised how beautifully the flavors came together.

2 pounds seasonal wild mushrooms, cleaned and sliced

3 leeks, white parts only, rinsed well and sliced crosswise

1 large onion

6 cloves garlic, minced

1 cup dry white wine

2 quarts chicken or seafood stock (pages 8 and 12)

$1/4$ cup flour

$1/4$ cup unsalted butter

Kernels cut from 6 ears fresh corn (about 5 cups)

1 pound cooked crabmeat or other seafood (such as scallops or prawns), or chicken (page 119)

2 tablespoons chopped fresh basil

1 tablespoon cayenne sauce

Salt

Freshly ground black pepper

In a large stockpot over medium heat, combine the mushrooms, leeks, onion, and garlic. Cover the pot and cook until the onion is tender, 5 to 8 minutes. Add the wine and reduce over high heat until $1/2$ cup liquid remains, about 5 minutes. Add the stock, bring to a boil, and reduce the heat to low.

Make a beurre manié by mixing together the flour and the butter. Ladle 2 cups of the simmering stock into a bowl and whisk in the beurre manié. Whisk the mixture back into the stock and simmer 25 to 30 minutes, or until the flavors are well blended. Add the corn and simmer briefly to blanch, about 5 minutes. Stir in the crab, basil, and cayenne sauce, and season with salt and pepper to taste. Ladle into bowls and serve piping hot.

fall squash soup

WITH CHORIZO AND SPICY CINNAMON CROUTONS

Serves 6 to 8

Mark made this soup on his first day at the Bistro, and it's the reason he's still there today.

1 medium-sized butternut, Hubbard, sweetmeat, or other fall squash, peeled, seeded, and cut into large dice

2 tablespoons olive oil, plus 1 teaspoon

1 tablespoon unsalted butter

2 large onions, cut into large dice

6 cloves garlic

1 cup marsala or dry sherry

8 cups chicken stock (page 8)

1 pound chorizo

1 tablespoon Worcestershire sauce

1 tablespoon cayenne sauce

2 teaspoons chopped fresh thyme

2 teaspoons chopped fresh oregano

Salt

Freshly ground black pepper

Spicy cinnamon croutons (page 13)

Preheat the oven to 350°. Place the squash on a roasting pan, toss it to coat with 2 tablespoons of the olive oil, and bake until tender and slightly caramelized, 25 to 30 minutes.

Heat the butter in a large stockpot over medium-high heat until hot. Add the onions and sauté until tender and browned. Add the garlic, roasted squash, and marsala, and cook over high heat until reduced by one-half. Add the stock, bring to a boil, reduce the heat to low, and simmer 10 to 15 minutes.

Meanwhile, heat the remaining teaspoon of olive oil in a sauté pan over medium-high heat. Add the chorizo, cook until it is well browned, and then drain the fat well.

Strain the squash and stock mixture through a fine sieve. Purée the solids and return the purée to the stockpot. Stir in the chorizo, Worcestershire sauce, cayenne sauce, thyme, and oregano, and season to taste with salt and pepper.

To serve, ladle the soup into individual soup bowls and garnish with the cinnamon croutons.

yellow tomato and garbanzo bean soup
WITH CUCUMBER-YOGURT SAUCE

Serves 6 to 8

One of the best things about summer is the vine-ripened tomatoes, especially since there are so many kinds available these days. Make this soup with your favorite variety.

2 tablespoons olive oil

5 pounds vine-ripened yellow tomatoes or red tomatoes, cored and coarsely chopped

1 large onion, cut into large dice

2 shallots, minced

8 cloves garlic, minced

2 cups dry white wine

8 cups chicken or vegetable stock (pages 8–9)

1 cup canned garbanzo beans

2 tablespoons finely chopped fresh oregano

2 teaspoons ground cumin

1 tablespoon rice wine vinegar

2 tablespoons cayenne sauce

Salt

White pepper

Cucumber-yogurt sauce, for garnish (page 15)

Heat the olive oil in a stockpot over medium-high heat until hot. Sauté the tomatoes, onion, shallots, and garlic until the onions are tender, 5 to 8 minutes. Add the wine and cook over high heat until the liquid is reduced by one-half. Add the stock and bring to a boil. Reduce the heat to low and simmer 30 minutes.

Add half of the garbanzo beans and the oregano, cumin, vinegar, and cayenne sauce. Strain the soup through a fine sieve. Purée the solids and return the mixture to the stockpot over medium heat. Stir in the remaining garbanzo beans and cook until heated through, about 5 minutes. Season to taste with salt and white pepper.

To serve, ladle the soup into individual serving bowls and garnish with cucumber-yogurt sauce.

sweet potato and caramelized onion soup

Serves 6 to 8

Roasted sweet potatoes and caramelized onions make a perfect match in this soup.

5 medium sweet potatoes, peeled and
   diced

3 tablespoons olive oil

1/4 pound pepper bacon, diced

5 large onions, julienned

3 cloves garlic, minced

1 cup dry white wine

8 cups chicken stock (page 8)

1 tablespoon Worcestershire sauce

1 tablespoon cayenne sauce

Salt

Freshly ground black pepper

Crème fraîche, for garnish (page 122)

Rosemary croutons, for garnish
   (page 13)

Preheat the oven to 350°. Toss the sweet potatoes with oil to coat and place them on a large sheet pan. Bake the sweet potatoes until they are tender and slightly caramelized, 45 minutes to 1 hour.

In the meantime, in a large stockpot over medium heat, add the bacon and cook until crispy. Remove the bacon, crumble, and reserve for garnish. Add the onions to the rendered bacon fat and cook, stirring occasionally, until they are golden brown and caramelized, 15 to 20 minutes.

Add the garlic and wine, and cook over medium-high heat until the liquid is reduced. Add the sweet potatoes and stock, and bring to a boil. Decrease the heat to low and simmer 25 to 30 minutes.

Purée the soup in a food processor or blender and return it to the pot. Stir in the Worcestershire sauce and cayenne sauce, and season to taste with salt and pepper.

To serve, ladle into individual serving bowls and garnish with the bacon, crème fraîche, and croutons.

bistro potato soup

W I T H   T A P E N A D E

Serves 6 to 8

Potato soup is such a hot seller at the Bistro that Jeff, one of our lunch cooks, ladles it nonstop during the entire service. A versatile soup, it can be made with any combination of stock and garnishes; seafood stock with shrimp or fish and asparagus stock with blanched asparagus tips and watercress purée are two of our favorites.

2 tablespoons olive oil

3 medium onions, julienned

6 cloves garlic, minced

1 cup dry white wine

5 pounds red or yellow potatoes, peeled
   and cut into large dice

8 cups chicken stock (page 8)

2 tablespoons balsamic vinegar

1 teaspoon cayenne sauce

1 pound Gorgonzola, crumbled

Salt

Freshly ground black pepper

Tapenade (page 15)

Heat the olive oil in a large stockpot over medium-high heat until hot. Sauté the onions and garlic until tender, 5 to 8 minutes. Add the wine and reduce over high heat until $^1/_4$ cup liquid remains, about 5 minutes.

Add the potatoes and stock, and bring to a boil. Reduce the heat to low. Cover the pot and simmer 25 to 30 minutes, or until the potatoes are tender. Strain the mixture through a fine sieve. Purée the solids and return the mixture to the pot. Bring the soup back to a simmer and stir in the vinegar, cayenne sauce, and half of the Gorgonzola. Season to taste with salt and pepper.

To serve, ladle into individual soup bowls and garnish with the remaining Gorgonzola and the tapenade.

split pea soup

WITH TASSO HAM AND ANDOUILLE SAUSAGE

Serves 6 to 8

Mark adds spicy Southern touches to give typical split pea soup a makeover.

1¹/₂ pounds dried split peas, sorted and
    rinsed

8 cups chicken stock (page 8) or water

2 tablespoons olive oil

1 large onion, diced

2 carrots, peeled and diced

2 stalks celery, diced

6 cloves garlic, minced

1 pound tasso ham, diced

1 pound andouille sausage, halved
    lengthwise and cut into ¹/₄-inch slices

1 cup dry white wine

1 teaspoon chopped fresh thyme or
    oregano

1 tablespoon cayenne sauce, or to taste

1 tablespoon Worcestershire sauce

Salt

Freshly ground black pepper

Crème fraîche, for garnish (page 122)

Roasted red bell pepper purée, for
    garnish (page 118)

In a large stockpot over medium-high heat, bring the split peas and stock to a boil. Reduce the heat to low and simmer 45 minutes to 1 hour, or until the peas are soft.

Meanwhile, heat the olive oil in a large sauté pan over medium-high heat until hot. Sauté the onion, carrots, celery, and garlic until fragrant and tender, 5 to 8 minutes. Add the ham and sausage, and cook until well browned, about 10 minutes.

Add the wine and cook over high heat until the liquid is reduced by one-half. Stir the vegetable mixture into the split peas and adjust the thickness of the soup with water or additional stock, if necessary. Add the thyme, cayenne sauce, and Worcestershire sauce, and season to taste with salt and pepper.

To serve, ladle the soup into bowls and garnish with crème fraîche and red bell pepper purée.

bistro chowder

Serves 6 to 8

Everyone should have a good basic chowder recipe, since this year-round favorite is easily adapted to the catch of the day or whatever's fresh from the garden. One of Mark's favorite variations is made with sweet potatoes and smoked trout.

8 cups fish stock (page 12) or clam juice

1/2 pound bacon, diced

1/2 cup flour

3 tablespoons olive oil

2 large onions, diced

1 bulb fennel, diced

2 stalks celery, diced

2 tablespoons garlic, minced

2 cups dry white wine

2 tablespoons cayenne sauce

2 tablespoons Worcestershire sauce

5 or 6 red potatoes, peeled and diced

6 cups half-and-half

Salt

Freshly ground black pepper

Bring the stock to a boil in a large stockpot over medium-high heat. Reduce the heat and simmer.

Meanwhile, in a large sauté pan over medium-high heat, cook the bacon until crispy. Remove the bacon and set aside, reserving the bacon fat for making a roux.

To make a roux, pour 1/2 cup of the rendered bacon fat into a small saucepan over medium heat. Stir in the flour and cook, stirring often, until the mixture is light brown and fragrant, 4 to 6 minutes.

Whisk the roux into the stock. Increase the heat to medium and cook 40 to 45 minutes, or until reduced by one-third.

Meanwhile, heat the olive oil in a large sauté pan over medium-high heat until hot. Sauté the onions, fennel, celery, and garlic until the fennel is tender, 5 to 8 minutes. Add the wine, cayenne sauce, and Worcestershire sauce, and cook over high heat until reduced by one-half. Add the potatoes to the stock mixture and simmer until tender, about 10 to 12 minutes. Stir in the sautéed vegetables and half-and-half, and season to taste with salt and pepper. Serve hot.

onion soup

WITH SCALLION-ROQUEFORT CROUSTADES

Serves 6 to 8

The scallion-Roquefort croustades make this classic onion soup even classier.

2 tablespoons unsalted butter

1 white onion, julienned

1 yellow onion, julienned

1 red onion, julienned

6 shallots, sliced

6 leeks, white parts only, rinsed well and
    sliced crosswise

3 cloves garlic, minced

1 cup dry white wine

2 tablespoons Dijon mustard

2 tablespoons balsamic or rice wine
    vinegar

6 cups chicken stock (page 8)

6 cups beef stock (page 9)

1 tablespoon Worcestershire sauce

1 dash Madeira or marsala

Salt

Freshly ground black pepper

1 bunch chives, chopped, for garnish

Scallion-Roquefort croustades,
    for garnish (page 14)

Melt the butter in a large stockpot over medium heat. Add the white, yellow, and red onions and the shallots, and cook, stirring often, until they have browned and caramelized, 35 to 45 minutes. Add the leeks and garlic, and cook until the leeks are tender, 5 to 8 minutes. Add the wine and cook over high heat until reduced by one-half. Add the Dijon mustard, vinegar, and stock. Bring the soup to a boil, decrease the heat to low, and simmer 20 to 25 minutes.

Stir in the Worcestershire sauce and Madeira, and season to taste with salt and pepper. To serve, ladle the soup into bowls and garnish with chives and croustades.

BREADS & Spreads

Like soup, the sandwich is rooted in humble, yet global, beginnings: falafel-stuffed pita bread, tortillas filled with beans, flatbread topped with smoked fish, or simple chunks of bread supporting pieces of hand-crafted cheese. Certainly the earl of Sandwich wasn't the first to eat his meat, cheese, and vegetables between two pieces of bread, but he gets the credit for popularizing the concept of this portable meal.

Over the years, sandwiches have taken on different personalities and styles. What was considered to be fancy finger food in the 1950s would now be considered merely two pieces of white bread spread with often boring ingredients. Luckily for us, with today's sandwiches anything goes—from meatloaf with cayenne aioli, to crostini topped with roasted vegetables and Gorgonzola, to delicate and pretty shrimp sandwiches with mango relish. Although sandwiches will always be lunchtime favorites, they now serve as unique breakfasts and satisfying dinner entrées. In the winter, John and I like to cook a roast and use it to make big ol' French dip sandwiches. And in the summer, it's barbecued burgers for large groups of friends.

Sandwiches are highlighted on the Bistro lunch menu, and we prepare a unique sandwich of the day using fresh seasonal ingredients. Our inspiration might come from a crate of beautiful heirloom tomatoes brought in that morning, which we'll quickly turn into a spicy tomato chutney to sit atop a barbecued salmon fillet. Sometimes ultra-fresh spot prawns start the creative process, and by the start of lunch, they may be transformed into a curried prawn sandwich topped with Chinese mustard. Whatever the raw materials, we always strive to offer customers something better than "just a sandwich." Our daily challenge is to create a sandwich with a pairing of flavors that can't be found any place else. And no matter what the sandwich of the day may be, you will never see the exact same item repeated on our menu.

In the following pages are master recipes that will help you build brilliant sandwiches from the ground up.

breads

A truly good sandwich begins with a loaf of excellent bread, such as nutty whole wheat, rich challah or brioche, crusty French, or dark, dense rye. Make the bread yourself—you'll enjoy the process almost as much as you'll like biting into the sandwich it will become. If you have the time, make several loaves at once, baking what you'll eat right away and freezing the remainder. When freshly baked bread sounds good, simply thaw a loaf overnight in the refrigerator and let it rise fifteen minutes or so while the oven heats.

If time just isn't on your side, purchase quality retail breads. Artisan bakeries abound these days, and there are plenty of hearty, rustic loaves to choose from. After building your sandwich, freeze any leftover bread, or make it into croutons, crostini, or bruschetta to serve with soup.

roasted shallot–herb brioche

Makes 2 loaves

- **6 shallots, peeled**
- **¹/₄ cup olive oil**
- **¹/₄ cup sugar**
- **2 tablespoons active dry yeast**
- **4¹/₂ cups all-purpose flour**
- **1 cup milk**
- **1 cup butter**
- **5 eggs**
- **2 tablespoons chopped basil, thyme, rosemary, or other fresh herbs**
- **2 teaspoons salt**

Preheat the oven to 300°. Place the shallots on a small ovenproof pan, drizzle with the olive oil, and bake 40 to 50 minutes, until soft. Remove the shallots from the oven and set aside to cool.

In a large bowl or mixer, combine the sugar, yeast, and 1¹/₂ cups flour. In a saucepan, heat the milk and butter until warm and the butter is melted, about 110°. With the mixer on low speed or while mixing by hand, slowly add the warm milk mixture. Beat the mixture about 2 minutes. Scrape down the bowl. Add the eggs and then the remaining flour, 1 cup at a time, mixing well after each addition.

Chop the roasted shallots and add them, along with the herbs and salt, to the flour mixture. Mix well, about 5 minutes. Place the dough in a well-greased large bowl and turn the dough in the bowl to lightly grease all over. Allow the dough to rise about 1 hour, or until doubled in size. Punch down the dough. Grease the dough again, cover, and refrigerate overnight.

The next day, punch the dough down again. Let the dough rest 15 minutes, then divide the dough in half and pat or roll each half out into a 9 x 5-inch rectangle. Starting on the long end, roll each rectangle into a tight roll, pinching along the seams to seal. Tuck the ends under the loaves and pinch again to seal. Place each loaf in a well-greased 9 x 5-inch loaf pan, cover, and allow to rise about 1 hour.

Place the loaves in a 350° oven and bake until they are golden brown, about 1 hour. Cool before slicing.

Variations

Ginger Brioche: Omit the roasted shallots. Add 2 tablespoons of chopped ginger to the milk-and-butter mixture before heating. Proceed with the recipe.

Garlic Brioche: Omit the roasted shallots. Add 20 cloves of roasted garlic when the herbs are added.

Toasted Walnut Brioche: Add 1¹/₂ cups toasted, chopped walnuts when the herbs are added.

honey wheat bread

Makes 2 loaves

    3 cups warm water
    4 tablespoon active dry yeast
    2 tablespoons olive oil
    1/2 cup honey
    1 cup oat bran
    1 cup wheat bran
    2 cups warm milk
    4 cups whole-wheat flour
    6 cups all-purpose flour
    2 tablespoons salt

In a bowl, mix together the water, yeast, and honey. Set aside until the mixture becomes foamy, about 5 to 10 minutes. Add the olive oil and mix well.

Place the oat and wheat bran in a mixer fitted with a dough hook. Add the yeast mixture and blend together. Add the warm milk and mix again. With the mixer running slowly, add the wheat and all-purpose flour. If the mixture seems too moist, add a bit more flour. When the flour is incorporated, add the salt. Run the mixer another 5 minutes, until a soft, smooth dough forms.

Place the dough in a large greased bowl, cover, and allow the dough to rise until doubled in size, 1 to $1^1/_2$ hours.

Punch the dough down and split it into 2 pieces. Pat or roll each half out into a 9 x 5-inch rectangle. Starting on the long end, roll each rectangle into a tight roll, pinching along the seams to seal. Tuck the ends under the loaves and pinch again to seal. Place each loaf in a well-greased 9 x 5-inch loaf pan.

Cook the loaves in a 375° oven until golden brown, about 1 hour. Let loaves cool before slicing.

garlic and herb flatbread

Makes about 8 rounds

1³/₄ cups warm water

1 tablespoon sugar

1 tablespoon active dry yeast

2 tablespoon olive oil

5 to 6 cups all-purpose flour

1 tablespoon salt

2 tablespoon olive oil

2 cloves garlic, minced

2 tablespoons chopped fresh basil,
   rosemary, thyme, or other herbs

Mix the water, sugar, and yeast in a mixing bowl or mixer, and let stand until foamy, about 10 minutes. Add the olive oil and mix. Add the flour, 1 cup at a time, mixing well after each addition. When all the flour has been incorporated, add the salt and mix until you have a shaggy dough.

Remove the dough from the mixer or bowl, and knead it on a well-floured board until it is smooth and elastic. Place the dough in a large greased bowl, cover, and allow the dough to rise until doubled in size, 1 to 1¹/₂ hours.

Punch the dough down and cut it into 8 pieces. Flatten the pieces with your hand to form 4- to 5-inch pizzalike rounds of dough.

Place the rounds on two well-greased sheet pans. Drizzle the dough with olive oil and sprinkle the chopped garlic and herbs over the rounds. Place the sheet pans in a 425° oven and bake the breads until golden brown, about 15 minutes. Remove from the oven and serve warm or cold.

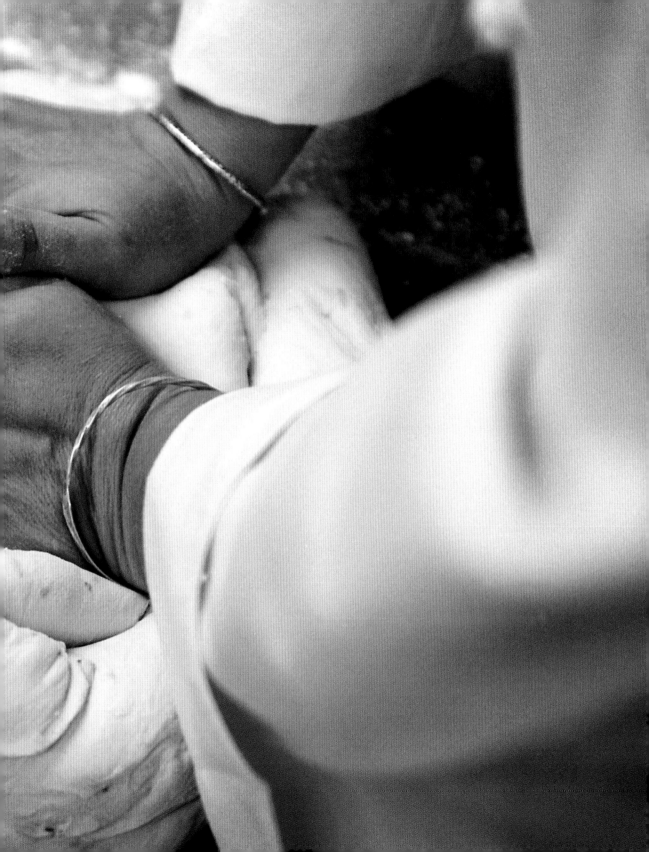

basic french bread
Makes 2 loaves or about 6 rolls or buns

3 cups warm water

2 tablespoons active dry yeast

2 tablespoons olive oil

6 to 7 cups all-purpose flour

1 tablespoon salt

Mix the water and yeast in a bowl or mixer, and let stand until foamy, about 10 minutes. Add the olive oil and mix well. Add the flour 1 cup at a time, while mixing, until you form a shaggy dough. Add salt and mix well.

Place the dough on a well-floured board and knead until it is smooth and elastic, about 10 minutes.

Place the dough in a large greased bowl, cover, and allow the dough to rise until doubled in size, 1 to 1¹/₂ hours.

Punch the dough down and split it into 2 pieces. Form the dough into 2 round loaves or 6 small round rolls or buns.

Place the dough on a well-greased sheet pan, cover with a kitchen towel, and let rise until doubled in size, about 1 hour.

Place in a 375° oven and bake until golden brown, about 1 hour for the loaves and 45 minutes for the buns. Let cool before slicing.

Variations

Olive and Basil French Bread: Add 2 cups chopped cured olives, such as kalamatas, and 2 tablespoons chopped fresh basil when olive oil is added.

Rosemary French Bread: Add 2 tablespoons chopped fresh rosemary when olive oil is added. (Other fresh herbs, such as thyme or oregano, can be substituted for the rosemary.)

focaccia

Makes 1 sheet pan

- **1 tablespoon active dry yeast**
- **2¹/₂ cups warm water**
- **2 tablespoons olive oil**
- **6 to 7 cups all-purpose flour**
- **1 tablespoon salt**
- **¹/₄ cup extra-virgin olive oil**
- **3 cloves garlic, chopped**
- **1 tablespoon cracked black pepper**
- **1 teaspoon kosher salt**

Mix the water and yeast in a bowl or a mixer, and let stand until foamy, about 10 minutes. Add the olive oil and mix well. Add the flour 1 cup at a time, mixing well after each addition until you form a shaggy dough. Add the salt and mix well.

Place the dough on a well-floured board and knead it well until it is smooth and elastic, about 10 minutes.

Place the dough in a large greased bowl, cover, and allow the dough to rise until doubled in size, about 1 hour.

Punch the dough down and form it into a 9 x 11-inch rectangle to fit a sheet pan.

Place the dough on a well-greased sheet pan, cover with a kitchen towel, and let the dough rise until doubled in size, about 1 hour.

Brush the dough with extra-virgin olive oil and top it with the chopped garlic, pepper, and kosher salt.

Place in a 400° oven and bake until golden brown, about 40 minutes. Remove the bread from the oven and invert it so the bottom doesn't get soggy. Serve warm or cold.

bistro rye bread

Makes 2 loaves

- ¹/₄ cup unsalted butter
- 1 tablespoon sugar
- ³/₄ cup milk
- ¹/₄ cup espresso or extra-strong coffee
- 2 tablespoons active dry yeast
- 2 tablespoons olive oil
- 4 cups all-purpose flour
- 4 cups rye flour
- 3 tablespoons caraway seeds
- 1 tablespoon salt

Place the butter, sugar, milk, and espresso in a saucepan, and heat to just under 110°. Mix with the yeast in a mixing bowl or a mixer and let stand until foamy, about 10 minutes. Add the olive oil. With the machine running or while mixing, add in both the flours, 1 cup at a time, until a shaggy dough forms. Add the caraway seeds and salt, and mix well.

Place the dough on a rye-floured board and knead until it is smooth and elastic, about 10 minutes.

Place the dough in a large greased bowl, cover, and allow the dough to rise until doubled in size, about 1 hour.

Punch the dough down. Grease the bowl again, cover, and let stand until doubled, about 1 hour.

Remove the dough from the bowl and cut the dough into 2 pieces. Pat or roll each half out into a 9 x 5-inch rectangle. Starting on the long end, roll each rectangle into a tight roll, pinching along the seams to seal. Tuck the ends under the loaves and pinch again to seal. Place the loaves in 2 well-greased 9 x 5-inch loaf pans. Cover and let stand for 30 minutes.

Place in a 375° oven and bake until golden brown, about 1 hour. Let cool before slicing.

...and spreads

To make a sandwich really stand out, you need brightly flavored and interesting spreads. Sandwiches at the Bistro are accented with herb purées, topped with mushroom-hazelnut duxelles, or drizzled with aioli that we spruce up with sundried tomatoes, Chinese mustard, fresh herbs, or roasted peppers. Since these spreads and condiments are quick and easy to make, the variety of recipes in this book should keep your mind off plain old mustard and mayonnaise for a long time.

What follows are a few of the Bistro's staple sandwich toppings. It's by no means an exhaustive selection, though, and you should feel free to incorporate garnishes and toppings from the soups chapter (or your own pantry!) as the inspiration strikes you.

green goddess dressing

Makes 2 cups

Green goddess is an old-fashioned dressing that is the perfect complement to the sweet, smoky Grilled Black Forest Ham Sandwich (page 105). It also blends nicely with the Roasted Chicken Tortilla Wrap (page 107).

- **2 tablespoons tarragon vinegar**
- **2 cloves garlic**
- **1 egg yolk**
- **2 tablespoons freshly squeezed lemon juice**
- **2 anchovy fillets**
- **1 teaspoon chopped fresh tarragon**
- **1 tablespoon chopped fresh flat-leaf parsley**
- **2 scallions, minced**
- **1 1/2 cups extra-virgin olive oil**
- **1/4 cup sour cream**
- **Salt**
- **Freshly ground black pepper**

Combine in a food processor the vinegar, garlic, egg yolk, lemon juice, anchovies, herbs, and scallions. Run the processor and drizzle the olive oil through the feed tube. Transfer the sauce from the processor to a bowl . Fold in the sour cream and season with salt and pepper. Refrigerate until ready to use.

balinese sambal

Makes 1 cup

I think I could put this sambal on top of just about anything, but on top of a barbecued pork sandwich, it is heaven. Try it on everything from grilled fish to a chicken breast. This sambal also intensifies the flavor of the Spicy Peanut Soup (page 39).

> 1 red bell pepper, roasted, peeled, seeded, and julienned (page 118)
> 1 Anaheim pepper, roasted, peeled, and seeded (page 118)
> 2 cloves garlic, chopped
> 1/2 cup toasted sweetened coconut
> 1 teaspoon chopped fresh basil
> 1 tablespoon rice vinegar
> Zest and juice of 1 lime
> 1 teaspoon fish sauce
> 1 teaspoon sweet soy sauce
> 1 tablespoon vegetable oil
> Salt
> Freshly ground black pepper

Place all the ingredients except the salt and pepper in a bowl and toss together. Season to taste with salt and pepper and refrigerate until ready to use.

roasted shallot shmear

Makes 1 1/2 cups

This is John's recipe, and we just love to smear it on everything! When the shallots and garlic are roasted, they become very rich, sweet, and mellow.

> 10 whole shallots, peeled and halved
> 10 cloves garlic
> 1/4 cup olive oil
> 1/4 cup balsamic vinegar
> 2 anchovies
> 2 tablespoons chopped fresh rosemary
> Salt
> Freshly ground black pepper

Preheat the oven to 300°. Place the shallots and garlic in an ovenproof pan, drizzle with the olive oil, and roast until the shallots are soft to the touch, 50 minutes to 1 hour. Purée the shallot mixture in a food processor. With the machine running, add the vinegar, anchovies, and rosemary, and purée until smooth. Season to taste with salt and pepper, and mix well. Refrigerate until ready to use.

herb-cheese spread

Makes 2 cups

When you make this cheese mixture, be sure to use herbs that are in season. If you have an herb garden, try using a variety of herbs, and just use this recipe as a guide.

 3 cloves garlic
 1 tablespoon each chopped fresh
  rosemary, basil, and thyme
 1 cup cream cheese
 1/2 cup soft mild goat cheese
 1/2 cup grated parmesan
 Salt
 Freshly ground black pepper

In the bowl of a food processor, combine the garlic, herbs, cream cheese, goat cheese, and parmesan, and process until smooth. Season to taste with salt and pepper. Refrigerate until ready to use.

blue cheese–scallion spread

Makes 1 cup

This blue cheese spread served on top of a rare seared piece of tuna makes for a perfect sandwich. It also adds a nice tangy flavor to Mark's Onion Soup (page 58).

 1 bunch scallions, green part only
 1 cup blue cheese
 1 teaspoon chopped fresh tarragon

Place all the ingredients in a food processor and process until smooth. Refrigerate until ready to use.

BISTRO Sandwiches

Lamb Burgers with Fennel Jam on Rosemary Buns / 76

Stuffed Portobello Mushroom Sandwich / 77

Roasted Sweet Pepper Sandwich on Roasted Shallot–Herb Brioche / 79

Seared Tuna Sandwich with Chinese Mustard Aioli / 80

Barbecued Pork Loin Sandwich with Balinese Sambal / 81

Bistro Burger / 83

Curry Roasted Leg of Lamb Sandwich with Baba Ghanouj / 84

Italian Sausage Sandwich with Ricotta-Herb Spread / 85

Meatloaf Sandwich with Cayenne Aioli / 87

Roasted Pork Tenderloin Sandwich with Pear Compote / 88

Spicy Catfish Sandwich with Tomato Relish / 92

Shrimp Sandwich with Mango Relish / 95

Open-Faced Ratatouille Sandwich / 96

Roasted Turkey Sandwich with Tomato Jam / 97

Grilled Steak Sandwich with Blue Cheese Sauce / 98

Bistro Rueben Sandwich with Three-Mustard Aioli / 99

Oyster Po' Boy / 101

Grilled Cod Sandwich with Crispy Pancetta and Mushroom-Hazelnut Duxelles / 102

Three-Cheese Sandwich with Garlic-Herb Spread / 103

Grilled Black Forest Ham Sandwich with Green Goddess Dressing / 105

Seared Tuna Sandwich with Blue Cheese–Scallion Spread / 106

Roasted Chicken Tortilla Wrap with Tabbouleh / 107

Hummus with Tomato-Cucumber Relish and Greek Olives / 109

Five-Spice Marinated Chicken Sandwich with Peanut Sauce / 110

Salmon Club Sandwich with Roasted Shallot Shmear / 111

Fish Cake Sandwich with Daikon-Carrot Salad / 113

lamb burgers

WITH FENNEL JAM ON ROSEMARY BUNS

Serves 6

*This recipe is a favorite at the Bistro. The
fennel jam is a versatile condiment—you can
serve it with grilled chicken or tuna, and it's
great tossed with pasta.*

fennel jam

1 teaspoon olive oil

1 onion, julienned

1 medium bulb fennel, julienned

1 large clove garlic, chopped

1/8 cup ouzo (anise-flavored liqueur)

1/8 cup brown sugar or cane sugar

Kosher salt

Freshly ground black pepper

2 tablespoons olive oil

1 1/2 small onions, minced

2 cloves garlic, chopped

2 pounds ground lamb

2 teaspoons chopped fresh oregano

1 teaspoon chopped fresh thyme

1/2 teaspoon freshly ground black pepper

Salt

6 rosemary French buns (see page 68)

3/4 cup soft mild goat cheese

1 large vine-ripened tomato, sliced

1/2 small red onion, thinly sliced

To prepare the jam, heat the olive oil in a large
nonstick sauté pan until smoking hot. Add
the onions and fennel, and do not stir until
they start to brown, 5 to 7 minutes. Toss and
allow the onions and fennel to brown, 5 to
7 minutes. Continue cooking until the onions
and fennel are caramelized, 10 to 15 minutes.
Purée the mixture in a food processor.

In a saucepan over low heat, combine the
purée, garlic, ouzo, and brown sugar, and
cook until thickened, 8 to 10 minutes. Season
to taste with salt and black pepper. Set aside.

To prepare the sandwich, heat 1 tablespoon
of the olive oil in a small sauté pan over high
heat until very hot. Sauté the onions and garlic
until fragrant, about 2 minutes. Let cool.

In a medium bowl, mix together the
ground lamb, cooled onion mixture, oregano,
thyme, and black pepper. Form the mixture
into 6 patties and season with salt.

Heat the remaining tablespoon of olive oil
in a large sauté pan over high heat until
lightly smoking. Add the lamb patties and
sear well, 3 to 4 minutes per side.

Split the French buns in half and spread
fennel jam on each roll. Top with a lamb
patty, goat cheese, tomato, and sliced onion,
and serve warm.

stuffed portobello mushroom sandwich

Serves 6

Portobellos are so incredibly meaty and flavorful that you won't even notice that this is
a vegetarian sandwich. The robust mushrooms, combined with the rich cheese filling,
make this sandwich very satisfying.

6 (5- to 6-inch) portobello mushrooms
Salt
Freshly ground black pepper
1 cup soft mild goat cheese
$^1/_3$ cup grated Asiago cheese
2 cloves garlic, chopped
$^1/_4$ cup oil-packed sundried tomatoes,
    drained and minced
1 tablespoon chopped fresh basil
2 teaspoons chopped fresh oregano
1 tablespoon olive oil
6 rosemary French buns (page 68)
Basil purée (page 14)
2 ounces mesclun mix

Preheat the oven to 425°. Remove the stems
from the mushrooms, then season with salt
and pepper to taste.

To prepare the filling, combine the goat
cheese, Asiago, garlic, tomatoes, basil,
oregano, salt, and pepper in a large bowl, and
mix well. Spoon the filling into the mushroom caps.

Pour the olive oil in a large roasting pan
and heat in the oven until smoking hot. Place
the mushrooms filling-side up in the pan and
roast until tender, 15 to 20 minutes. During
the last 5 minutes of roasting time, split the
buns and toast them in the oven.

Remove the mushrooms and buns from
the oven. Place a mushroom on each roll,
drizzle with a bit of the basil purée, and top
with mesclun mix. Serve warm.

roasted sweet pepper sandwich
ON ROASTED SHALLOT–HERB BRIOCHE

Serves 6

This vegetarian sandwich takes advantage of the rich flavor of sweet peppers paired with creamy, pungent fontina and the crisp bite of arugula. It's a great sandwich to enjoy for lunch or dinner while you sit on your deck and sip a glass of wine.

12 slices roasted shallot–herb brioche
   (page 63)

2 tablespoons olive oil

2 heads roasted garlic (page 118)

4 red bell peppers, roasted, peeled,
   seeded, and julienned (page 118)

4 yellow bell peppers, roasted, peeled,
   seeded, and julienned (page 118)

10 ounces sliced fontina cheese

2 tablespoons basil purée (page 14)

Salt

Freshly ground black pepper

$1/4$ pound fresh arugula

Brush each slice of the brioche with olive oil and grill or toast the bread until golden brown. Spread each slice with the roasted garlic. Place the roasted peppers on 6 slices of the bread. Top with the fontina, drizzle with basil purée, and season with salt and pepper. Top each sandwich with the arugula and another slice of bread. Cut the sandwiches on an angle and serve.

seared tuna sandwich

WITH CHINESE MUSTARD AIOLI

Serves 6

Topped with a spicy, crispy cabbage salad, this sandwich is full of flavor and great textures. Be sure to keep from overcooking the tuna. If it's overcooked, it becomes dry and tasteless. If tuna isn't available, try another firm fish, such as sturgeon or cod, or even try chicken.

cabbage salad

2 cups thinly sliced red cabbage

2 cloves garlic, chopped

1 teaspoon chopped, peeled fresh ginger

2 tablespoons freshly squeezed lemon
   juice

¼ cup vegetable oil

2 tablespoons sweet hot chile sauce

1 teaspoon dark sesame oil

1 teaspoon curry powder, toasted
   (page 120)

Soy sauce

6 (4-ounce) tuna fillets

1 tablespoon vegetable oil

Salt

Freshly ground black pepper

6 French rolls (page 68)

¼ cup Chinese mustard aioli (page 121)

To prepare the cabbage salad, place the cabbage in a large bowl and set aside. In a mixing bowl, combine the garlic, ginger, and lemon juice. Slowly whisk in the vegetable oil until emulsified. Add the chile sauce, sesame oil, and curry powder, and mix well. Pour the dressing over the cabbage and toss well. Season to taste with soy sauce and set aside.

To prepare the tuna, heat the oil in a large sauté pan over high heat until lightly smoking. Season the tuna with salt and pepper, and sear it 2 minutes per side (the fish will be very rare). Split the French rolls in half, and place a tuna fillet on each roll. Top with Chinese mustard aioli, cabbage salad, and the top half of the roll. Cut in half and serve warm.

barbecued pork loin sandwich
WITH BALINESE SAMBAL

Serves 6

Sambal is an intensely flavored chile condiment. Our recipe, which has a fresher taste than the bottled version, has coconut and lime. The barbecue sauce can keep for weeks in your refrigerator. Try it on ribs or grilled chicken.

yummy asian barbecue sauce

1 tablespoon olive oil

1 small onion, minced

3 cloves garlic, chopped

1 tablespoon chopped, peeled, fresh
  ginger

1 cup mirin

$^1/_4$ cup honey

$^1/_2$ cup hoisin sauce

$^1/_2$ cup tomato purée

$^1/_4$ cup fermented black beans

2 teaspoons chile paste

2 tablespoons rice vinegar

Soy sauce

3 pounds boneless pork loin

Salt

Freshly ground black pepper

2 teaspoons olive oil

6 French rolls (page 68)

Balinese sambal (page 72)

To prepare the barbecue sauce, heat the olive oil in a saucepan over high heat until very hot. Sauté the onion, garlic, and ginger until fragrant, about 2 minutes. Add the mirin and reduce over high heat until about $^1/_4$ cup of liquid remains. Add the honey, hoisin, tomato purée, fermented black beans, chile paste, and vinegar, and cook over medium heat until thick, about 10 minutes. Season to taste with soy sauce and refrigerate until ready to use.

To prepare the sandwiches, preheat the oven to 300°. Season the pork loin with salt and pepper.

Heat the olive oil in a large ovenproof sauté pan over high heat until smoking hot. Place the pork loin in the pan and sear well on all sides, 3 to 4 minutes per side. Remove the pork loin from the heat and brush it generously with the barbecue sauce.

Transfer the pork loin to the oven and cook 35 to 45 minutes for medium doneness. Remove the pork loin from the oven and let it stand about 3 minutes. Slice it very thin.

Split each French roll in half and distribute the meat on each roll. Drizzle with barbecue sauce, and top with sambal. Serve warm.

bistro burger

Serves 6

This is our classic burger with the delicious addition of smoked onions. Be creative in your own kitchen by adding roasted garlic or shallots to the burger mixture, or by adding a different kind of fresh herb.

2 teaspoons olive oil

2 shallots, chopped

3 cloves garlic, chopped

1 large smoked onion (page 119), diced

2¹/₂ pounds ground beef

1 teaspoon Worcestershire sauce

2 teaspoons cayenne sauce

2 teaspoons chopped fresh thyme

Kosher salt

Freshly ground black pepper

12 ounces Gorgonzola or other blue cheese, Cheddar, or your favorite cheese

6 French buns (page 68)

Herb aioli (page 121)

1 large vine-ripened tomato, sliced

1 large red onion, sliced

6 leaves lettuce

Heat the olive oil in a sauté pan over high heat until very hot. Sauté the shallots, garlic, and smoked onion until tender, about 5 minutes.

Remove the onion mixture from the heat and let it cool completely.

In a large bowl, combine the ground beef, cooled onion mixture, Worcestershire sauce, cayenne sauce, and thyme. Mix well and form into 6 patties, then season them with salt and pepper.

Oil the grill and heat until very hot. Grill the patties 3 to 4 minutes per side, or until they are done to your liking. During the last 2 minutes of cooking, top each patty with a slice of cheese.

Split each French bun in half and spread the aioli on each bun. Then top the bun with a patty, the tomato and onion slices, and a lettuce leaf. Serve immediately.

Note: To guard against *E. coli*, cook the hamburgers to 160° internal temperature (well done).

curry roasted leg of lamb sandwich

WITH BABA GHANOUJ

Serves 6

This is a long-time favorite sandwich at the Bistro. Chris, our lunch cook at the Bistro, is the king of baba ghanouj and hummus. Sometimes when he prepares them in the morning for a lunch special, we eat them for breakfast.

baba ghanouj

1 medium eggplant

³/₄ cup tahini paste

3 cloves garlic, chopped

¹/₄ cup extra-virgin olive oil

Juice of 1 lemon

2 teaspoons toasted, ground cumin
(page 120)

Salt

2¹/₂ to 3 pounds boneless leg of lamb

Salt

Freshly ground black pepper

2 tablespoons curry paste

2 tablespoons olive oil

6 rounds garlic and herb flatbread
(page 65)

2 medium vine-ripened tomatoes, sliced

To prepare the baba ghanouj, preheat the oven to 425°. Place the eggplant on a roasting pan and roast it for about 40 minutes, or until soft.

Remove the eggplant from the oven and peel off the skin when it is cool enough to handle.

Place the eggplant, tahini paste, and garlic in a food processor, and purée until smooth. With the machine running, slowly add the olive oil. Stop the machine. Add the lemon juice, cumin, and salt, and run the machine to mix. Set aside.

To roast the lamb, preheat the oven to 300°. Clean the leg of lamb of fat and silvery skin, roll it up, and tie it with butcher's twine to secure. Season the lamb with salt and pepper, and rub with curry paste.

Heat the olive oil in an ovenproof sauté pan over high heat until smoking hot. Add the lamb and sear well on all sides, 3 to 4 minutes per side.

Transfer to the oven and roast the lamb 45 to 50 minutes for medium doneness. Let sit about 3 minutes then slice very thin.

To finish the sandwiches, cut the flatbread in half. Spread 6 pieces with baba ghanouj, layer with sliced lamb and tomato slices, and top with the remaining flatbread. Serve warm.

italian sausage sandwich
WITH RICOTTA-HERB SPREAD

Serves 6

Use a good-quality, whole-milk ricotta in the herb spread (fat-free ricotta won't taste nearly as good). You can also serve the spread tossed with fresh spaghettini for a quick, tasty pasta dish.

ricotta-herb spread

1¼ cups ricotta cheese

2 cloves garlic, chopped

1 tablespoon chopped fresh basil

1 teaspoon chopped fresh thyme

1 teaspoon chopped fresh oregano

¼ cup finely grated Parmesan cheese

2 scallions, minced

Salt

Freshly ground black pepper

2 tablespoons olive oil

3 red bell peppers, julienned

2 tablespoons balsamic vinegar

2 pounds bulk Italian sausage

6 French rolls (page 68)

To prepare the herb spread, mix together the ricotta, garlic, basil, thyme, oregano, Parmesan, scallions, salt, and pepper in a medium bowl. Set aside.

Heat 1 tablespoon of the olive oil in a large sauté pan over high heat until very hot. Add the bell peppers and cook until tender, about 5 minutes. Add the balsamic vinegar and remove from the heat.

Form the sausage into 6 patties. Heat the remaining tablespoon of olive oil in a large sauté pan over high heat until hot. Place the sausage patties in the pan and cook 3 minutes per side, or until cooked through.

Split the French rolls in half, and place a sausage patty on each roll. Then top with sautéed peppers, the ricotta-herb spread, and the top half of the roll. Serve warm.

meatloaf sandwich
WITH CAYENNE AIOLI

Serves 6

Juicy, well-seasoned meatloaf, spicy aioli, and thick slices of grilled onion—a welcome change from the typical meatloaf sandwich. This is one of John's all-time favorites.

meatloaf

2 teaspoons olive oil

3 cloves garlic, chopped

1 small red onion, minced

3 pounds ground beef

2 eggs

¹/₄ cup fresh bread crumbs (page 120)

1 teaspoon tomato paste

1 teaspoon Worcestershire sauce

1 tablespoon cayenne sauce

1 teaspoon dried thyme

1 teaspoon dried basil

1 teaspoon dried rosemary

2 teaspoons salt

1 tablespoon freshly ground black pepper

6 large slices of onion

12 thick slices honey wheat bread (page 64)

6 slices extra-sharp Cheddar

1 large vine-ripened tomato, sliced

Cayenne aioli (page 121)

To prepare the meatloaf, preheat the oven to 350°. Heat the olive oil in a sauté pan over high heat until very hot. Sauté the onion and garlic until tender, about 2 minutes. Set aside to cool completely.

In a large bowl, combine the ground beef, cooled onion mixture, and eggs, and mix well. Add the bread crumbs, tomato paste, Worcestershire sauce, cayenne sauce, herbs, salt, and pepper, and mix well.

Place the mixture in a loaf pan and bake in the oven for 45 to 50 minutes, or until cooked through. Remove the meatloaf from the oven and let it cool in the pan for about 10 minutes. Remove from the pan and slice.

Over a hot grill, cook the onion slices 3 to 5 minutes per side, or until tender. Place slices of meatloaf on 6 pieces of the bread. Top with a slice of cheese, grilled onion, tomato, and the cayenne aioli. Top with another slice of bread, and cut the sandwiches in half. Serve warm.

roasted pork tenderloin sandwich

WITH PEAR COMPOTE

Serves 6

When making the pear compote, use pears
that aren't too ripe. You want them flavorful,
but firm enough so they won't fall apart.
Pecans and walnuts both make tasty variations for the nut spread.

pear compote

2 teaspoons olive oil

2 shallots, chopped

3 cloves garlic, chopped

1 small red onion, julienned

3 large pears, peeled and sliced

1/2 cup dry sherry

1 tablespoon chopped fresh tarragon

2 tablespoons rice vinegar

1 tablespoon brown sugar

Salt

1 teaspoon freshly ground black pepper

nut spread

**1/2 cup hazelnuts, toasted and skins
removed (page 120)**

3/4 cup cream cheese

2 tablespoons milk

2 cloves garlic

1 tablespoon Dijon mustard

4 dashes Tabasco sauce

Salt

Freshly ground black pepper

2 pounds pork tenderloin, cleaned

Salt

Freshly ground black pepper

**12 slices roasted shallot–herb brioche
(page 63)**

1 tablespoon olive oil

To prepare the pear compote, heat the olive
oil in a large sauté pan over high heat until
very hot. Sauté the shallots, garlic, and red
onion until fragrant, about 2 minutes. Add the
pears and toss to combine. Add the sherry and
cook over high heat until most of the liquid is
reduced, 3 to 4 minutes. Add the tarragon,
vinegar, and brown sugar, and cook until the
sugar dissolves, about 2 minutes. Season to
taste with salt and pepper, and set aside.

To prepare the nut spread, chop the hazelnuts in a food processor. Add the cream
cheese, milk, garlic, mustard, and Tabasco,
and process until smooth. Season to taste
with salt and pepper. Set aside.

To prepare the tenderloin, preheat the
oven to 350°. Season the pork with salt and
pepper. Heat the oil in a large ovenproof sauté
pan over high heat until smoking hot. Add
the tenderloin and sear well on all sides, 3 to
4 minutes per side. Transfer to the oven and

cook 5 to 8 minutes (depending on the thickness of the pork) for medium doneness. Remove from the oven and slice very thin.

Top 6 slices of the bread with several slices of tenderloin and top with pear compote. Spread the remaining slices of bread with nut spread and place on top of the sandwiches. Cut in half and serve warm.

spicy catfish sandwich
WITH TOMATO RELISH

Serves 6

Catfish has a mild, delicate flavor that lends itself well to hearty seasonings. We serve it often at the Bistro. I especially like it in this sandwich, with its spicy breading and a tangy tomato relish.

tomato relish

2 teaspoons olive oil

1 small red onion, julienned

2 cloves garlic, chopped

3 tomatoes, peeled, seeded, and
   diced (page 118)

$^1/_4$ cup oil-packed sun-dried tomatoes,
   drained and diced

2 jalapeños, roasted, peeled, and minced
   (page 118)

2 teaspoons tomato paste

$^1/_2$ cup red wine

1 tablespoon sherry vinegar

2 teaspoons chopped fresh thyme

6 dashes Tabasco sauce

Salt

Freshly ground black pepper

6 (4-ounce) catfish fillets or other firm
   whitefish (such as snapper)

Salt

Freshly ground black pepper

$^1/_2$ cup flour

2 teaspoons cayenne pepper

1 teaspoon garlic powder

2 teaspoons onion powder

$^1/_2$ teaspoon dried thyme

$^1/_2$ teaspoon oregano

1 tablespoon olive oil

12 slices roasted garlic brioche (page 63)

$^1/_8$ pound fresh arugula

To prepare the relish, heat the olive oil in a large sauté pan over high heat until hot. Sauté the onion and garlic lightly until fragrant, about 2 minutes. Add the tomatoes and sauté until cooked through but still firm, about 4 minutes. Add the sundried tomatoes, jalapeños, and tomato paste, and toss to mix together. Add the red wine and reduce until about 1 tablespoon of liquid remains. Add the vinegar and thyme, and cook briefly, about 1 minute. Stir in the Tabasco sauce and season to taste with salt and black pepper. Remove from the heat and set aside.

To prepare the fish, preheat the oven to 350°. Season the fish with salt and pepper. In a medium bowl, mix together the flour, cayenne pepper, garlic powder, onion powder, thyme, and oregano. Transfer to a large plate. Dredge the fish well in the flour.

Heat the olive oil in a large ovenproof sauté pan over high heat until lightly smoking. Place the fish in the pan and cook until golden brown, about 3 minutes per side.

Transfer to the oven and bake just until done, 2 to 3 minutes, or longer if very thick. (If the fillets are less than 1 inch thick, you do not need to finish cooking them in the oven.)

Toast the brioche. Distribute the fish among 6 slices of the bread. Top with relish and arugula, and cover with the remaining slices of bread. Serve warm.

shrimp sandwich
WITH MANGO RELISH

Serves 6

Mango relish makes a tangy and refreshing topping for the rich, garlicky shrimp in this sandwich. If spot prawns are available in your area, try using them for the ultimate shrimp sandwich.

mango relish

- 2 mangoes, peeled and diced
- 1 small red onion, minced
- 1 tablespoon peeled, chopped fresh ginger
- 2 cloves garlic, chopped
- 1 tablespoon rice vinegar
- Juice of 1 lime
- 1 tablespoon chopped chives or garlic chives
- 1 teaspoon chile sauce
- Soy sauce
- 1 tablespoon vegetable oil

- 1 tablespoon vegetable oil
- 2 cloves garlic, chopped
- 1 tablespoon chopped, peeled, fresh ginger
- 2 teaspoons instant sour paste (optional)
- 24 large shrimp, cleaned and butterflied
- Pinch chile flakes

Soy sauce

12 slices roasted shallot–herb brioche (page 63)

1/4 cup Chinese mustard aioli (page 121)

1/8 pound mesclun mix

6 sprigs fennel or dill, for garnish

To prepare the relish, place the mangoes, red onion, ginger, and garlic in a bowl, and toss to mix together. Add the rice vinegar, lime juice, chives, and chile sauce, and mix well. Season with soy sauce to taste. Add the vegetable oil and toss well to coat. Set aside.

Heat the vegetable oil in a large sauté pan over high heat until smoking hot. Add the garlic, ginger, sour paste, and shrimp, and cook just until the shrimp turn pink, 1 to 2 minutes.

Remove from the heat and add the chile flakes and soy sauce.

Top 6 slices of the bread with about 4 shrimp each and drizzle with Chinese mustard aioli. Top with mango relish and mesclun mix. Then top with another slice of bread. Garnish with fennel or dill, and serve warm.

open-faced *ratatouille* sandwich

Serves 4

You can make the ratatouille several days in advance, and then gently warm it when you make the sandwich. To keep the ratatouille from becoming too mushy, be sure to cook the vegetables in order of firmness, the crisp ones first, the tender ones last.

ratatouille

1 tablespoon olive oil

3 cloves garlic, chopped

¹/₂ yellow onion, diced

1 small eggplant, diced

¹/₂ cup sliced portobello mushrooms

1 small yellow squash, diced

1 small zucchini, diced

2 tomatoes, halved, seeded, and diced (page 118)

2 red bell peppers, roasted, peeled, seeded, and diced (page 118)

2 teaspoons tomato paste

¹/₃ cup chopped cured olives

1 tablespoon chopped fresh basil

1 teaspoon chopped fresh oregano

Salt

Freshly ground black pepper

8 slices rosemary French bread (page 68)

¹/₂ cup sundried tomato crème fraîche (page 122)

8 slices mozzarella cheese

To prepare the ratatouille, heat the olive oil in a very large sauté pan over high heat until very hot. Sauté the garlic and onion until fragrant, about 2 minutes. Add the eggplant and sear about 3 minutes. Then toss and sear 3 minutes longer. Add the mushrooms, squash, zucchini, and tomatoes, and sauté until tender, about 4 minutes. Add the peppers and tomato paste, and stir well. Then add the olives and herbs, and cook for about 2 minutes. Season to taste with salt and pepper.

To prepare the sandwich, toast or grill the French bread. Then preheat the broiler. Distribute the ratatouille among the slices of bread. Spoon the sundried tomato crème fraîche onto each sandwich and top with a slice of cheese. Broil the sandwiches just until the cheese melts, about 3 minutes. Serve warm, 2 sandwiches per person.

roasted turkey sandwich
WITH TOMATO JAM

Serves 6

Tomato jam, with caramelized onion and reduced fresh tomato, has a sweet, rich flavor, making a nice contrast to the savory roasted turkey. The tomato jam is also a nice complement to the Mediterranean Vegetable Soup (page 31) and the Black Bean Soup with Chocolate (page 18).

tomato jam

1 tablespoon olive oil

2 onions, julienned

3 cloves garlic, chopped

1/2 cup dry sherry

1/2 cup red wine

4 tomatoes, seeded and chopped
(page 118)

1 tablespoon tomato paste

1/4 cup oil-packed sundried tomatoes,
drained and julienned

1 tablespoon brown sugar

Salt

Freshly ground black pepper

6 squares focaccia (page 69)

2 pounds sliced roasted turkey, home-
roasted or store bought (page 119)

6 large slices Gouda

2 tablespoons basil purée (page 14)

To prepare the jam, heat the olive oil in a large nonstick sauté pan on high heat until very hot. Add the onions and let them cook, without stirring, to caramelize, about 5 minutes. Toss the onions and continue cooking, without stirring, until the onions start to brown, 4 to 5 minutes. Continue to cook the onions until golden brown, another 6 to 8 minutes. Add the garlic and sauté quickly. Remove the onions and garlic from the pan and purée the mixture until smooth. Place the onions back in the pan. Add the sherry and red wine, and bring to a boil. Add the tomatoes, tomato paste, sundried tomatoes, and brown sugar, and cook until very thick, about 10 minutes. Season to taste with salt and black pepper. Set aside.

To prepare the sandwich, toast or grill the focaccia. Preheat the broiler. Place the turkey into 6 mounds on a lightly greased sheet pan. Top each mound with a slice of Gouda, and broil just until the cheese is melted.

While the turkey is broiling, split each square of focaccia and spread with tomato jam. Place each mound of turkey on a piece of focaccia, drizzle with basil purée, and top with the remaining focaccia. Cut the sandwiches in half and serve warm.

grilled steak sandwich
WITH BLUE CHEESE SAUCE

Serves 4

New York steaks aren't as tender as tender-loin, but they have a lot more flavor. I like to toss together spinach, the blue cheese sauce, and slices of steak to make a satisfying warm salad.

blue cheese sauce

$1/2$ **cup dry white wine**

2 cloves garlic, chopped

1 shallot, chopped

1 cup heavy whipping cream

1 teaspoon Dijon mustard

4 ounces blue cheese

2 teaspoons chopped fresh thyme

Salt

Freshly ground black pepper

$1^1/2$ **pounds New York steak**

Salt

Freshly ground black pepper

4 ($1/4$-inch-thick) slices yellow or sweet onion

2 teaspoons olive oil

2 teaspoons paprika

6 French rolls (page 68)

To prepare the blue cheese sauce, in a large saucepan over high heat combine the wine, garlic, and shallot, and reduce until about 2 tablespoons of liquid remain. Add the cream and reduce until about $1/3$ cup remains. Stir in the mustard and blue cheese, and mix well. Add the thyme and season to taste with salt and pepper. Keep warm until ready to use.

Season the steaks with salt and pepper. Toss the onion slices with the olive oil and sprinkle them with paprika, salt, and pepper. Oil the grill and heat until very hot. Place the onions on the grill and cook 3 to 4 minutes per side. Set aside.

Grill the steaks on the very hot grill 4 to 5 minutes per side, depending on the thickness of the steak, for medium-rare doneness. Let the steaks sit for 2 minutes, then slice the steaks very thin.

Split the French rolls in half, and place the sliced steak on each roll. Drizzle with the warm blue cheese sauce, and top with grilled onions. Cut in half and serve warm.

bistro reuben sandwich

WITH THREE-MUSTARD AIOLI

Serves 6

When Mark was the lunch chef, I used to beg him to make this sandwich as the special. It is, without a doubt, my favorite sandwich in the whole world.

> 2 pounds thinly sliced corned beef
>   (homemade or the best store bought)
> 12 slices Bistro rye bread (page 70)
> 1^1/$_2$ cups sauerkraut
> 6 large slices Jarlsberg or other Swiss
>   cheese
> ^{1}/$_3$ cup three-mustard aioli (page 121)
> ^{1}/$_4$ cup unsalted butter

To prepare the sandwiches, distribute the corned beef among 6 slices of the bread. Top the meat with the sauerkraut and a slice of cheese. Spread one side of each of the remaining slices of bread with aioli and place the slices on the sandwiches.

Heat 2 tablespoons of the butter in a very large sauté pan over medium-high heat. Add three of the sandwiches and cook on each side until brown, about 2 to 3 minutes per side. Remove from the pan and keep warm while cooking the remaining 3 sandwiches in the same manner.

Cut the sandwiches in half and serve warm.

oyster po' boy

Serves 4

The Northwest is known for its oysters, and at the Bistro we get our oysters from a southern Oregon grower. They are plump and juicy—some of the best in the state.

oyster flour

1 cup flour

¹/₂ cup cornmeal

2 teaspoons dried thyme

1 teaspoon dried oregano

2 teaspoons garlic powder

2 teaspoons onion powder

1 teaspoon salt

2 teaspoons freshly ground black pepper

20 freshly shucked oysters

2 tablespoons olive oil

4 French rolls (page 68)

¹/₄ cup cayenne aioli (page 121)

6 leaves romaine lettuce, julienned

To prepare the oyster flour, mix together the flour, cornmeal, thyme, oregano, garlic powder, onion powder, salt, and pepper in a bowl.

Transfer the oyster flour to a large plate, and dredge the oysters in the flour.

Heat the oil in one very large sauté pan or two medium sauté pans over high heat until lightly smoking. Add the oysters and cook just until they are browned, 3 to 4 minutes per side, depending on the size. Drain well on paper towels.

Split each French roll in half and place 5 oysters on each roll. Drizzle with cayenne aioli and top with lettuce. Serve warm.

grilled cod sandwich

WITH CRISPY PANCETTA AND MUSHROOM-HAZELNUT DUXELLES

Serves 6

Duxelles is a classic mushroom dish, often used as a stuffing or topping. Mark added toasted hazelnuts to it one night at the Bistro as an accompaniment to the fish special. I thought duxelles would taste great on a sandwich, so I paired it with a tender cod fillet and crispy pancetta. Duxelles also sits nicely on top of the Bistro Potato Soup (page 55).

mushroom-hazelnut duxelles

- 1¹/₂ tablespoons unsalted butter
- 1¹/₂ tablespoons olive oil
- 3 cups chopped cremini mushrooms
- 3 shallots, chopped
- 3 cloves garlic, chopped
- ¹/₃ cup dry sherry
- ¹/₂ cup toasted, skinned, and coarsely ground hazelnuts (page 120)
- Salt
- Freshly ground black pepper

- 6 thick slices pancetta
- 6 (4-ounce) cod fillets or other firm whitefish
- Salt
- Freshly ground black pepper
- 12 slices honey-wheat bread (page 64)
- 1 bunch watercress

To prepare the duxelles, heat the butter and olive oil in a large sauté pan over high heat until very hot. Sauté the mushrooms, shallots, and garlic briefly. Then reduce the heat to medium-low and sauté about 20 to 30 minutes, until the liquid from the mushrooms is gone. Add the sherry and cook over medium-high heat just until the sherry is reduced, about 4 minutes. Add the chopped hazelnuts. Season to taste with salt and pepper, and set aside.

To prepare the sandwich, preheat the oven to 350°. Place the pancetta on a lightly greased sheet pan and bake until crispy, 5 to 8 minutes. Remove the pancetta from the oven and drain on paper towels.

Season the cod with salt and pepper. Oil the grill and heat until very hot. Place the cod on the grill and cook one side 3 to 5 minutes. Turn the fish over, spread the cooked side with about ¹/₄ cup of the duxelles, and cook until the fish is just cooked through, 3 to 5 minutes, depending on the thickness.

Toast or grill the bread. Distribute the fish among 6 slices of the bread. Top with the crispy pancetta, watercress, and the remaining slices of bread. Serve warm.

three-cheese sandwich
WITH GARLIC-HERB SPREAD

Serves 6

The classic combination of cheese, garlic, and herbs tastes all the better when it's melted between sweet, tender roasted shallot–herb brioche. Try this sandwich with the rouille (page 15).

garlic-herb spread

1/4 cup extra-virgin olive oil

1 bunch basil

1 tablespoon chopped fresh rosemary

1 tablespoon chopped fresh thyme

1/4 cup grated Parmesan cheese

3 cloves garlic

12 slices roasted shallot–herb brioche
   (page 63)

6 large slices mozzarella

6 large slices Gouda

6 large slices fontina cheese

2 ripe plum tomatoes, sliced

3 tablespoons olive oil

To prepare the garlic spread, combine the olive oil, basil, rosemary, thyme, Parmesan, and garlic in a food processor, and process until smooth. Set aside.

Spread 6 slices of the bread with the garlic spread. Layer the sandwich with a slice of each of the cheeses. Top with the sliced tomatoes and the remaining slices of bread.

Brush both sides of each sandwich with olive oil. Heat a large nonstick pan over high heat until very hot. Place as many sandwiches in the pan as will fit and brown until the cheese melts, 3 to 5 minutes per side. Keep the finished sandwiches warm while the others cook. Cut in half and serve warm.

grilled *black forest* ham sandwich
WITH GREEN GODDESS DRESSING

Serves 6

This is a sandwich that will remind you of childhood, but with a much more grown-up flavor. The rich flavors of the ham and Gouda contrast nicely with the vibrant combination of fresh herbs, garlic, and lemon in the green goddess dressing.

- **2 pounds sliced good-quality Black Forest ham**
- **6 slices Gouda**
- **2 bunches arugula or watercress**
- **6 heaping tablespoons green goddess dressing (page 71)**
- **12 slices Bistro rye bread (page 70)**
- **2 tablespoons olive oil**

Distribute the ham onto 6 slices of bread. Top the ham with the cheese and arugula. Spoon the green goddess dressing over the arugula and top with the remaining slices of bread.

Heat 1 tablespoon of olive oil in a very large sauté pan over medium-high heat until hot. Add 3 of the sandwiches and cook on each side until brown, 2 to 3 minutes per side.

Remove from the pan and keep them warm while cooking the remaining 3 sandwiches in the same manner. Cut the sandwiches in half and serve warm.

seared tuna sandwich

WITH BLUE CHEESE–SCALLION SPREAD

Serves 4

This blue cheese–scallion spread is great on soup and spread on charred rare tuna, with its beef tenderloin-like texture. Since the tuna is served rare, be sure to use the best quality tuna.

4 (4- to 5-ounce) tuna fillets
Salt
Freshly ground black pepper
1 tablespoon olive oil
Blue cheese–scallion spread
    (page 73)
2 ounces fresh arugula
3 tablespoons lemon aioli (page 121)
4 squares focaccia, split (page 69)

Season the tuna fillets with salt and pepper. Heat the oil in a very large sauté pan over high heat until lightly smoking. Add the tuna fillets and cook just 2 minutes per side (the tuna will be very rare; do not overcook or it will become dry). Remove the tuna from the pan.

Split each square of focaccia in half and spread each piece with the blue cheese–scallion spread and aioli. Place each tuna fillet on a slice of focaccia and top with arugula and the remaining pieces of bread. Serve warm.

roasted chicken tortilla wrap
WITH TABBOULEH

Serves 6

This sandwich is filled with a tabbouleh salad that's a bit different from the traditional kind. I use less bulgur wheat and more fresh herbs, giving the sandwich an especially lively taste.

tabbouleh

1/3 cup chicken stock (page 8)

1/2 cup bulgur wheat

2 cloves garlic, chopped

1/4 cup freshly sqeezed lemon juice

2 tablespoons extra-virgin olive oil

1/2 cup chopped flat-leaf parsley

1/2 cup minced scallions

1/4 cup chopped fresh mint

1/2 small cucumber, peeled, seeded, and cut into small dice

2 plum tomatoes, seeded and cut into small dice (page 118)

Salt

Freshly ground black pepper

6 large flour tortillas

1 1/2 pounds roasted chicken, removed from the bone (page 119)

1/2 cup plain yogurt

1/2 cup feta cheese, crumbled

To prepare the tabbouleh, bring the chicken stock to a boil over medium-high heat. Place the bulgur in a large bowl. Pour the boiling chicken stock over the bulgur, cover with plastic wrap, and let sit for 10 to 15 minutes, or until all the liquid is absorbed.

In a bowl, whisk together the garlic, lemon juice, and olive oil. Add the parsley, scallions, mint, cucumber, and tomato, and mix well. Then stir the mixture into the bulgur. Season to taste with salt and pepper. Set aside.

To prepare the sandwiches, warm the tortillas. Place 1 tortilla on a cutting board. Place a loosely packed 1/2 cup of cooked chicken in the middle of the tortilla, then about 2 tablespoons each of the yogurt and crumbled feta. Top with 1/2 cup tabbouleh. Fold over one side of the tortilla to meet the middle and cover the filling. Fold in the two ends of the tortilla and roll it up. Keep the finished sandwiches warm while preparing the remaining sandwiches. Serve warm.

hummus *with tomato-cucumber relish*

AND GREEK OLIVES

Serves 6

Heather, our food stylist, loves this sandwich. Every time we shoot the television show, she threatens to strike unless we make this sandwich for lunch.

hummus

1¹/₂ cups canned garbanzo beans

³/₄ cup tahini paste

3 cloves garlic, chopped

Juice of 1 lemon

¹/₄ cup extra-virgin olive oil

2 teaspoons toasted, ground cumin
   (page 120)

Salt

cucumber-tomato relish

2 tomatoes, seeded and chopped
   (page 118)

1 small cucumber, peeled, seeded, and
   diced

1 teaspoon chopped, peeled fresh ginger

2 cloves garlic, chopped

1 shallot, chopped

2 tablespoons rice vinegar

2 tablespoons vegetable oil

¹/₂ teaspoon chile paste

1 teaspoon chopped fresh cilantro

Salt

Freshly ground black pepper

¹/₂ cup pitted, diced kalamata olives or
   other cured olives

6 leaves lettuce

6 French rolls or 6 squares focaccia,
   (pages 68–69)

To prepare the hummus, place the garbanzos, tahini paste, garlic, and lemon juice in a food processor, and process until smooth. With the machine running slowly, add the olive oil. Add the cumin and salt, and process until mixed. Set aside.

To prepare the relish, combine the tomatoes, cucumber, ginger, garlic, and shallot in a medium bowl. Add the vinegar, olive oil, chile paste, and cilantro. Season to taste with salt and pepper, and mix well. Set aside.

To prepare the sandwiches, split each French roll in half and spread each bottom half with hummus. Top with relish, chopped olives, lettuce, and the remaining pieces of bread. Cut the sandwiches in half and serve.

five-spice marinated chicken sandwich
WITH PEANUT SAUCE

Serves 6

This is the same peanut sauce we serve at the Bistro with our hot-as-hell chicken. Be sure to give yourself plenty of time to marinate the chicken. If you're short on time, however, just barbecue the chicken and top it with the peanut sauce.

6 (4- to 5-ounce) boneless, skinless
    chicken breasts
$^1/_2$ cup five-spice marinade (page 122)

peanut sauce

2 teaspoons chopped, peeled fresh
    ginger
2 teaspoons chopped fresh cilantro
2 cloves garlic, chopped
2 fresh jalapeño peppers, stems removed
$^1/_2$ cup red wine vinegar
$^1/_2$ cup soy sauce
1 heaping cup creamy peanut butter
2 teaspoons curry powder, toasted
    (page 120)
$^1/_4$ cup honey
2 teaspoons dark sesame oil

12 slices French bread (page 68), or
    6 large flour tortillas
1 small cucumber, peeled and very thinly
    sliced

In a nonreactive bowl, combine the chicken with the marinade. Cover with plastic wrap, refrigerate, and marinate at least 1 hour. Oil the grill and heat until very hot. Place the chicken on the grill and cook until just cooked through, 6 to 8 minutes, depending on thickness.

Meanwhile, prepare the peanut sauce. Combine the ginger, cilantro, garlic, peppers, vinegar, and soy sauce in a food processor, and process to chop. Add the peanut butter, curry, honey, and sesame oil, and process until smooth. Set aside.

Slice the chicken breasts and distribute among 6 slices of the bread. Top with peanut sauce, the sliced cucumbers, and remaining slices of bread. Alternatively, wrap the chicken slices, peanut sauce, and cucumber in tortillas. Serve warm.

salmon club sandwich

WITH ROASTED SHALLOT SHMEAR

Serves 6

This is definitely not your traditional club sandwich. John's roasted shallot shmear makes all the difference. It's great on everything, from toasted French bread to turkey sandwiches.

  2 tablespoons olive oil

  6 slices pancetta

  6 (4-ounce) salmon fillets

  Freshly ground black pepper

  Kosher salt

  18 slices Bistro rye bread or French
     bread (pages 70 and 68)

  1/3 cup roasted shallot shmear (page 72)

  1/3 cup herb-cheese spread (page 73)

  1/4 pound fresh arugula, cleaned

Heat 1 tablespoon of the olive oil in a medium sauté pan over high heat until hot. Add the pancetta and cook until it is crispy, about 3 to 5 minutes.

Season the salmon with the black pepper and salt. Heat the remaining tablespoon of olive oil in a large sauté pan over high heat until smoking hot. Place the salmon in the pan and sear well, 3 to 4 minutes per side, depending on the thickness. Remove the salmon from the heat.

Toast or grill the bread. Spread 6 slices of the toasted bread with some of the roasted shallot shmear. Top each slice with a piece of seared salmon. Place another slice of toasted bread on top of the salmon. Spread each slice with herb-cheese spread, then top with a slice of pancetta and some arugula. Top each sandwich with another slice of toasted bread. Cut the sandwiches on an angle and serve warm.

fish cake sandwich

WITH DAIKON-CARROT SALAD

Serves 6

I know the number of ingredients in this sandwich is a bit scary, but don't shy away from this recipe. It's a favorite on the appetizer list at the Bistro and well worth the extra work to knock the socks off your friends.

daikon-carrot salad

2 carrots, finely julienned

1 small daikon radish, julienned

2 tablespoons rice vinegar

2 cloves garlic, chopped

2 teaspoons peeled, chopped fresh
  ginger

4 tablespoons vegetable oil

2 teaspoons chopped cilantro

1 teaspoon chile sauce

Soy sauce

2 teaspoons olive oil

1 teaspoon sesame oil

1 jalapeño, seeded and minced

1 shallot, chopped

2 teaspoons chopped ginger

1 tablespoon very finely minced lemongrass

2 cloves garlic, chopped

1 tablespoon instant sour paste

$^1/_3$ cup dry sherry

1 teaspoon curry powder, toasted
  (page 120)

1 teaspoon turmeric

$^1/_2$ teaspoon galangal powder

1 pound sea scallops

1 pound cod, halibut, or other whitefish,
  diced

$^1/_3$ cup fresh bread crumbs (page 120)

1 egg

$^1/_2$ cup sweetened coconut

2 teaspoons chopped cilantro

2 scallions, minced

$^1/_3$ cup pickled ginger, chopped, plus
  $^1/_3$ cup whole, for garnish

1 teaspoon salt

Flour or dried unseasoned bread crumbs,
  for dredging

4 tablespoons Chinese mustard aioli
  (page 121)

6 large slices ginger brioche (page 63),
  toasted and halved diagonally

6 sprigs cilantro, for garnish

continued from page 113

To prepare the carrot salad, place the julienned carrot and daikon in a bowl, and set aside.

In a small bowl, combine the rice vinegar, garlic, ginger, vegetable oil, cilantro, and chile sauce. Mix well and add soy sauce to taste. Pour over the julienned vegetables and mix well. Let marinate at least 30 minutes.

To prepare the cakes, heat the olive and sesame oils in a sauté pan over high heat until very hot. Lightly sauté the jalapeño, shallot, ginger, lemongrass, and garlic, about 2 minutes. Add the sour paste and toss to mix well. Add the sherry and reduce for 1 minute. Add curry, turmeric, and galangal, and cook 2 to 3 minutes. Remove the mixture from the heat and refrigerate until cool to the touch.

Place the scallops and diced whitefish in a food processor. Process until smooth (you may have to stop the machine and scrape down the sides once or twice). Transfer the mixture to a large bowl. Add the bread crumbs, eggs, cooled spice mixture, coconut, cilantro, scallions, chopped ginger, and salt. Mix well.

Form the mixture into 12 two-inch patties and dredge them in flour or bread crumbs.

To finish the sandwich, heat a large ovenproof sauté pan with olive oil until smoking hot. Add the cakes and brown them well on both sides, about 2 to 3 minutes. Place the cakes in a 400° oven for another 5 minutes. Remove from the oven.

Spread a bit of the Chinese mustard aioli on each triangle of bread and top each with a fish cake. Place two of the triangles on each plate and top each with $^1/_3$ cup of the daikon-carrot salad. Garnish with pickled ginger and cilantro, and serve warm.

THE Basics

peeled tomatoes

Bring a stockpot of water to a boil and prepare an ice-cold water bath. Cut an X in the bottom of each tomato. Add the whole tomatoes to the stockpot and blanch briefly, 1 to 2 minutes. Using a slotted spoon, transfer the tomatoes to the water bath. When cool, place the tomatoes on a work surface and peel.

seeded tomatoes

Cut the tomatoes in half crosswise. Cup one tomato half in the palm of your hand and gently squeeze until the seeds spill out.

roasted bell peppers and chiles

Peheat the broiler. Place the peppers or chiles on a baking sheet and broil, turning until the skins are evenly blistered and charred, about 15 minutes. Transfer to a bowl, cover with plastic wrap, and set aside to cool. When they are cool enough to handle, peel off the skins, remove the stems, and wipe the seeds away. Do not rinse the peppers or chiles under running water because this washes away much of the roasted flavor. Use as directed or drizzle with olive oil and store in an airtight container in the refrigerator for up to 2 months.

roasted red bell pepper purée

Makes about 1 cup

> **2 red bell peppers, roasted, peeled, and seeded**
> **1 clove garlic**
> **1/2 cup extra-virgin olive oil**
> **Salt**
> **Freshly ground black pepper**

Place all the ingredients in a food processor and purée until smooth. Season to taste with salt and pepper. Refrigerate until ready to use.

roasted garlic

> **1 head garlic**
> **2 tablespoons olive oil**

Preheat the oven to 250°. Slice about 1/4- inch off the top of the garlic head and discard. Drizzle the oil over it and wrap in foil. Roast until soft, 40 to 50 minutes. Roasted garlic will keep in the refrigerator for 2 to 3 weeks.

roasted garlic purée

Makes about 1 cup

> **1/2 cup extra-virgin olive oil**
> **2 heads roasted garlic**
> **Salt**
> **Freshly ground black pepper**

Pour the oil into a food processor. Squeeze the cooled garlic out of each head and into the oil. Process until the garlic is smooth. Season to taste with salt and pepper. Keep refrigerated until ready to use.

smoked onions

Smoking is an easy process that can be done up to 5 days before you want to use the onions. Use large yellow onions.

Prepare coals by piling briquettes on one side of the barbecue and lighting them. Let them burn until they are gray in color. Meanwhile, peel and cut the onions in half. Remove the grill from the barbecue and spray it with an oil spray. Place smoking chips (alder, apple, grape vines, tea, or any type of hardwood) on the coals, and put the grill back on the barbecue. Place the onions flat side down on the opposite side of the grill from the coals. Cover the barbecue and let the onions smoke for 1 to 2 hours, adding more chips if the smoke dies down. Onions should be nicely browned and have a lightly smoked aroma.

cooked lobster tail and crayfish

Bring a large pot of water to a boil over high heat. Add the lobster tail or crayfish and boil until the shells turn pink, about 7 to 8 minutes for the lobster and 4 to 5 minutes for the crayfish, depending on their size. Remove the lobster or crayfish from the shells and use as directed.

roasted chicken

Preheat the oven to 350°. Season the chicken with salt and pepper, and place on a roasting pan. Place the chicken in the oven and roast for 1 to $1\frac{1}{2}$ hours, depending on the size of the chicken, until it reaches an internal temperature of 150°. Remove from the oven and let stand for 5 minutes before slicing.

cooked crab

Bring a large pot of water to boil over high heat. Add the whole cleaned crab and cook about 10 minutes. Remove the crab from the pot and cool. Remove the meat and use as directed.

roasted turkey breast

Preheat the oven to 350°. Tie the boneless turkey breast to secure. Season with salt and pepper, and place in a roasting pan. Roast the turkey until it reaches an internal temperature of 150°, 1 to $1\frac{1}{4}$ hours, depending on the size of the breast. Remove from the oven and let stand for 5 minutes before slicing.

blanched and shocked
vegetables

Bring a large pot of water to a boil over high heat. Add vegetables and cook until crisp-tender. Drain immediately and place in ice-cold water to stop the cooking process. Use as directed.

cooked white rice

Makes about 4 cups

> 2 cups long-grain white rice
> 2¹/₂ tablespoons vegetable oil
> 2 teaspoons salt
> 2 quarts water

Rinse the rice in a colander under cold running water until the water runs clear and then drain. Place the rice, oil, salt, and water in a saucepan over medium-high heat, and bring to a boil. Continue to boil, uncovered, until almost all of the water has cooked off, 10 to 12 minutes. Stir the rice, cover, decrease the heat to low, and simmer for 8 to 10 minutes. Remove the rice from the heat and fluff with a fork just before serving.

toasted spices

To toast spices, place the whole or ground spices in a dry skillet over medium-low heat and toast while stirring continuously. Toast whole spices about 2 minutes, ground spices about 3 to 5 minutes, or until they begin to brown and are aromatic. Remove from the heat and set aside to cool.

toasted nuts

To toast nuts, place them on a baking sheet and toast in a 350° oven for about 10 minutes, or until they are golden brown and aromatic. Let cool completely, then use as directed.

skinned hazelnuts

To skin hazelnuts, toast them (see directions above), then wrap the hazelnuts in a kitchen towel and set aside to cool. When completely cool, leave the nuts wrapped in the towel and vigorously roll them between your palms until most of the skins have been removed. (It is not necessary to remove all the skins.) Use as directed.

bread crumbs

Makes about 2 cups

Remove the crust from 5 slices of white bread and discard. Place the bread in a food processor and process until fine. Remove and store in an airtight container.

lemon aioli

Makes about 2 cups

Aioli is an essential ingredient to a great sandwich, and once you get the hang of the lemon aioli you will see its possibilities are endless. Aioli can also be drizzled over broth-style soups to perk up the flavor.

Juice of 1 lemon

1 tablespoon Dijon mustard

$^1/_4$ cup white wine vinegar

2 anchovy fillets

2 cloves garlic

2 egg yolks

1$^1/_2$ cups extra-virgin olive oil

Salt

Freshly ground black pepper

To prepare the aioli, place the lemon juice, mustard, vinegar, anchovies, garlic, and egg yolks in the bowl of a food processor. Process until smooth. With the motor running, drizzle the olive oil through the feed tube until the aioli is thick and smooth. Season to taste with salt and pepper. Refrigerate until ready to use.

Variations

Herb Aioli: Add 2 tablespoons chopped fresh herb of your choice to the lemon aioli before adding the olive oil.

Cayenne Aioli: To the lemon aioli, add $^1/_4$ cup cayenne sauce with the olive oil.

Chinese Mustard Aioli: To the lemon aioli, fold in $^1/_4$ cup of Chinese mustard. Soften the aioli with just enough warm water to form a paste. Instead of salt, season with soy sauce and omit the black pepper.

Three-Mustard Aioli: To the lemon aioli, add 2 tablespoons whole-grain mustard and 2 tablespoons green peppercorn mustard.

crème fraîche

2 cups heavy whipping cream
2 tablespoons sour cream

In a small bowl, combine the whipping cream and sour cream, and mix well. Cover and let sit at room temperature overnight. Refrigerate.

Variations

Sundried Tomato Crème Fraîche

1 cup crème fraîche
2 cloves garlic, chopped
1/2 cup oil-packed sundried tomatoes, drained

Place the crème fraîche in a bowl and set aside. Place the garlic and sundried tomatoes in a food processor, and process until smooth. Add the mixture to the crème fraîche and stir well. Chill until ready to use.

five-spice marinade

Makes about 1/4 cup

2 teaspoons salt
2 teaspoons sambal oelek
2 tablespoons five-spice powder
2 cloves garlic, mashed
1 tablespoon soy sauce

In a small bowl, combine all ingredients and mix well. Refrigerate until ready to use.

Glossary of Terms and Ingredients

Arugula: Also called rocket, arugula is a tender green with a nutty, spicy flavor. I like to add it to salads, sandwiches, and pastas.

Blanch: To partially cook briefly in boiling water.

Bok Choy *(and baby bok choy)*: Also called Chinese white cabbage, bok choy is a dark green cabbage that somewhat resembles Swiss chard; baby bok choy is a smaller, more tender variety.

Butterfly: To cut a piece of meat nearly all the way through and open it out to make it twice as long but half as thick as it originally was. The meat should then be pounded flat with a meat mallet.

Caramelize: To cook sugar or an ingredient with a naturally high sugar content (such as some vegetables and meats) over high heat to brown the natural sugars and develop a deeper flavor.

Cayenne sauce: A vinegar-based, tangy, spicy sauce. I like to add it to soups, sauces, marinades, and salsas.

Chile paste: A Chinese condiment made from fermented fava beans, red chiles, and, sometimes, garlic.

Chorizo sausage: A spicy Mexican sausage made with pork and beef, seasoned with chile. Available in specialty markets and many supermarkets.

Crème fraîche: Cream combined with sour cream (or buttermilk) that is left out at room temperature for 8 to 24 hours, then refrigerated until thickened.

Crystallized ginger: Also known as candied ginger. Available in most grocery stores and in Asian markets.

Curry paste: A mixture of ghee (clarified butter), vinegar, and curry powder used to flavor Indian and Asian dishes. Sold in gourmet and specialty shops.

Daikon: A large Asian radish with white flesh that is juicy, sweet, and crisp.

Emulsify: To completely blend together an oil or fat with an acid such as vinegar or lemon juice.

Fermented black beans: Small black soybeans preserved with salt. They have a distinct pungency and strong salty taste. Widely used in Chinese cooking, I rinse them before using.

Fish sauce: A thin sauce made from fermented salted sardines or other fish.

Galangal powder: Galangal is a member of the ginger family. The powder has a piquant taste somewhat like cardamom and ginger.

Instant sour paste: A potent Asian flavoring paste that adds complexity to many dishes. I prefer the Tom Yum brand, which I use like salt and pepper. It keeps indefinitely in the refrigerator.

Julienne: Cut into matchsticks about $1/8$ inch across by 2 inches long.

Kalamata olives: Smooth-skinned, dark purple, brine-cured Greek olives with an intense taste.

Kosher salt: Pure salt with an even, coarse texture; more soluble than table salt. Available in specialty markets and most supermarkets.

Lemongrass: A standard herb in Vietnamese and Thai cooking. Use fresh lemongrass for cooking; dried lemongrass is mainly used for tea. Available in Asian markets and some supermarkets.

Mesclun: Mixed wild salad greens.

Nonreactive bowl/pan/container: Made of glass, ceramic, or stainless steel. Metal components in aluminum and cast-iron can react with the acids in ingredients resulting in an off flavor.

Palm sugar: Coarse unrefined sugar that is made from the sap of palm trees or sugar cane juice.

Pancetta: Unsmoked, peppered Italian bacon. Available in gourmet markets.

Parchment paper: Oil- and moisture-resistant paper used to line baking sheets and pans to prevent baked items from sticking.

Pickled ginger: A common Japanese condiment, it consists of very thinly sliced ginger pickled in rice vinegar, salt, and spices. Commercial varieties are artificially colored.

Prosciutto: Dry-cured, spiced Italian ham available in gourmet markets.

Reduce: To thicken and intensify the flavor of a sauce by boiling it down.

Sambal: An Indonesian spicy-hot pepper relish used as a flavoring or condiment.

Sambal oelek: A basic type of Indonesian sambal that includes chiles, salt, and brown sugar.

Shock: To submerge briefly in ice-cold water to stop the cooking process.

Tahini: A paste made from toasted sesame seeds that is used in Middle Eastern cooking.

Tamarind pulp: Sweet-sour paste made from the fruit of the pods of the tamarind tree.

Tapenade: A thick paste made from capers, anchovies, black olives, olive oil, and lemon juice.

Tasso ham: A lean, cured piece of pork or beef seasoned with spices, red pepper, and garlic, then smoked for about 2 days.

Thai basil: A basil variety with green and maroon leaves that has a slightly spicy flavor.

Wasabi: Japanese green mustard, with similar flavor and usages as horseradish. Wasabi is very hot and pungent, and should be used sparingly. Available in powder and paste form in Asian markets and some supermarkets.

Wild mushrooms: All edible, nonpoisonous mushrooms that are indigenous to certain areas throughout the Pacific Northwest, among other regions. Some of the most common are chanterelles, enoki, morels, and shiitakes, which are all known for their particularly earthy qualities.

Index

Don't Miss the 3 Companion Volumes to Caprial's Public Television Cooking Series!

Caprial's Bistro-Style Cuisine

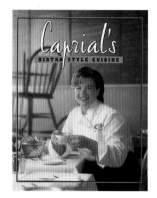

Caprial's culinary talents shine through in this collection of almost 200 recipes for starters, entrées, and desserts. Her creative spark and gift for clear instruction distinguish this beautiful volume, a must-have for the aspiring home chef. Color photographs throughout.

25,000 copies in print

**7 ³/₈ x 9 ¹/₈ inches • 208 pages
$24.95 cloth • ISBN 0-89815-946-6**

Available at your local bookstore, or order direct from the publisher. To order, or for more information, call 800-841-BOOK. Write or call for our free catalog of over 500 books, posters, and tapes.

1⊙ TEN SPEED PRESS
P.O. Box 7123 • Berkeley, CA 94707
800-841-BOOK
www.tenspeed.com

Cooking with Caprial
AMERICAN BISTRO FARE

Over 200 recipes for the earthy, down-home food that has earned Caprial's Portland, Oregon bistro a reputation as a destination restaurant. Color photographs throughout.

50,000 copies in print

**7 ³/₈ x 9 ¹/₄ inches • 224 pages
$24.95 cloth • ISBN 0-89815-788-9**

Caprial's Cafe Favorites

Caprial's first book, and the one that inspired and empowered countless readers to start the home range a-cookin'. The 130 recipes focus on reasonably priced fresh ingredients and hassle-free preparation. Color photographs throughout.

70,000 copies in print

**7 ³/₈ x 9 ¹/₄ inches • 160 pages
$21.95 cloth • ISBN 0-89815-600-9**